E A R T H   Q U E S T

The aim of the *Earth Quest* series is to examine and explain how shamanic principles can be applied in the journey towards self-discovery – and beyond.

Each person's Earth quest is the search for meaning and purpose in their life – it is the establishment of identity and the realization of inner potentials and individual responsibility.

Each book in the series examines aspects of a life science that is in harmony with the Earth and shows how each person can attune themselves to nature. Each book imparts knowledge of the Craft of Life.

Power within the Land

R. J. (Bob) Stewart is a Scottish author and composer, with thirty books in publication, translated into many languages worldwide. He works with myth, imagination, music, and the primal magical arts of inner change and vision. Bob has twenty years experience in theatre, film, television, recording and touring as a performer, with several award winning productions. For the last ten years he has concentrated mainly on writing and working with small groups in Europe and the USA, specifically working towards regenerating ancient traditions of inner transformation for practical modern use.

EARTH QUEST

Power within the Land

*The Roots of Celtic
and Underworld Traditions*

*Awakening the Sleepers
and Regenerating the Earth*

R. J. Stewart

ELEMENT

Shaftesbury, Dorset ● Rockport, Massachusetts
Brisbane, Queensland

© R. J. Stewart 1992

Published in Great Britain in 1992 by
Element Books Limited
Longmead, Shaftesbury, Dorset

Published in the USA in 1992 by
Element, Inc.
42 Broadway, Rockport, MA 01966

Published in Australia in 1992 by
Element Books Limited for
Jacaranda Wiley Limited
33 Park Road, Milton, Brisbane 4064

Reprinted 1993

Cover illustration by Miranda Gray
Cover design by Barbara McGavin
Illustrations by Miranda Gray
Diagrams by Taurus Graphics
Designed by Roger Lightfoot
Typeset by Footnote Graphics, Warminster, Wiltshire
Printed and bound in Great Britain by
Dotesios Ltd, Trowbridge, Wiltshire

British Library Cataloguing in Publication
data available

Library of Congress Cataloging in Publication
data available

ISBN 1–85230–331–X

Orchil

I dreamed of Orchil the dim goddess
Who is under the brown earth in a vast cavern
Where she weaves at two looms:
With one hand she weaves life upward through the grass,
With the other she weaves death downward through the mold.
And the sound of the weaving is eternity
And the name of it in the green world is time.
And through all, through all, Orchil weaves the weft
Weaves the weft of eternal beauty,
Orchil weaves the weft of eternal beauty,
Eternal beauty, that passeth not
Though its soul is change.

William Sharp writing as Fiona Macleod (text as set to music by John Foulds)

Author's Note to the Reader

There are powerful techniques and exercises in this book; please do not undertake them frivolously, as they work on deep levels of consciousness and energy. The Underworld tradition is not a substitute for therapy or medication. All practical use of the methods described in this book and in the companion volume *Earth Light* is your own sole responsibility, so consider it carefully before you begin. Reasons and motives for any inner or transformative work vary from person to person, but some of the valid aims for modern work within the Underworld tradition are listed in *How to Use This Book* (page xi).

The author cannot enter into detailed correspondence or give spiritual or psychological counselling. You may, however, write to R. J. Stewart, BCM 3721, London WC1N 3XX, with any reports of your experiences in the Underworld, enclosing a return-paid envelope. Replies are not guaranteed, and if they do occur may take several months to appear, so please be patient.

Contents

ACKNOWLEDGEMENTS

Before textual acknowledgements I should mention the many group members who have worked with me in the last ten years in Europe and the USA. Particular thanks, in no particular order, to the following friends, sources and inspirers: Deirdre Green, Gareth Knight, William G. Gray, Marko Galley, John and Caitlín Matthews, Ann Nielson, Philippa Keeling. The following pages do not represent their specific beliefs or opinions but my own interpretation of a venerable tradition. Traditional, spiritual and inner, yet historical and human contacts and sources include Robert Kirk, Thomas Rhymer, William Sharp, members of the Merlin tradition, and a host of bards, singers, story-tellers and Underworld and faery seers and seeresses whose names may never be known. I should also acknowledge my Welsh grandmother, whom I never met but who had the Second Sight.

The Grail as Bodily Vessel (Appendix 3) is reproduced by permission of Penguin Books; *The Hall in the Forest* (Chapter 8) and *An Underworld Journey* (Chapter 2) are reproduced from *Advanced Magical Arts* published by Element Books.

How to Use This Book

Power within the Land is designed to give the reader the means to experience the deeper levels of the Underworld and of the resulting relationship between humanity, other forms of life and the land that arises from Underworld spiritual work. In this sense the book stands alone, with various exercises suggested in a developing order (see page 122 for this sequence). For a broader picture of the tradition, the reader should refer to the first book *Earth Light* which examines the initiatory and transformative potential of faery lore within the Underworld.

Rather than repeat all of the basic exercises from the first book or constantly refer the reader back to it for practical work, alternative exercises are included in Chapter 2 and in the Appendices. These should be worked through before attempting the exercises and visualizations in the main text, and the programme suggested on page 122 will be helpful for your own development within the Underworld tradition, and for a gradual approach to the more powerful experiences. Two short essential exercises, one for basic visualization and one for attuning vital energies, are found in both books, reproduced here in Chapter 2. Part 2 of this book contains the main visions and other methods of working with the deeper levels of the Underworld.

You will certainly benefit from working with the material in *Earth Light* before you work with this book but I have tried to imagine, as far as the practical work goes, that there will be some people who have not done so. So although there are references in several chapters to material in the first volume, the experiential work stands alone and can be done without the first volume. It does not, however, replace or do away with knowledge and experience of the faery realm or make the first book irrelevant, for it travels instead along some of the variant paths found within the Underworld.

The branches or paths of the Underworld tradition interconnect in many ways and are often referred to as *realms*. The faery realm is one major path of interaction and experience, while the way of the Dark Goddess is another that underpins the entire tradition. *Power within the Land* offers some of the techniques and teachings of other realms and shows how these interact with us.

The way to use this book begins with reading text but eventually you will put the book away, having replaced it with your own experience and having developed skills from the practical exercises. First, I would suggest reading the book through from beginning to end, as you would a novel. Next, begin the practical work. Try to avoid the understandable urge to experiment with the visions or workings that immediately appeal to you, and follow instead the suggested programme of development.

If you have not worked with Underworld lore before, this programme is essential for balanced progress, though you may choose to vary the amount of time spent in each stage. If you have worked within the Underworld, either through the exercises in *Earth Light* or *The Underworld Initiation*, then I would suggest that you simply work through the programme until you reach material new to you, doing the earlier Underworld exercises once each. These earlier exercises are variants of the basic Underworld Initiation, but designed to attune to the deeper work described throughout this book.

After working through the series of basic exercises, you will probably want to refer back to specific chapters, using the index and glossary. Next, I would recommend reading the entire book through again for, after the practical work, you will find that much of the material in each chapter takes on new significance. If you are willing to keep a diary, then notes on one entire cycle of exercises can be enlightening when they are read at a later date: such note-taking often helps to fix details in the memory, especially in the short period after meditation, visualization or ritual. But the Underworld tradition is essentially one of experience rather than analysis and what you *become* is infinitely more valuable than what you write down.

WHO AND WHY?

Who are the Underworld beings and orders?
Why should we meet and work with them?

Power within the Land is about contact and awakening within and through the Underworld Initiation. The Underworld Initiation involves deep changes of consciousness through a series of mythic visions and leads to the realization of Earth Light, in which we discover that the world is alive and filled with light. This ancient yet vibrant spiritual tradition teaches that light and spiritual reality are found within the body of the sacred land and planet, and not exclusively far away or in higher dimensions. This idea is discussed in more detail in the later chapters.

Contact and awakening are mutual events and the practical work in the later chapters offers ways of bringing both about. But who do we contact through the Underworld tradition of spiritual interaction and transformation? How are we awakened, and who do we awaken? Why should we follow this path at all? Before attempting any of the theory or practice, we should be aware of these questions and try to answer them in a way that is suited to the modern psyche. As Underworld and Earth Light traditions are environmental, the details of the answers will vary from land to land but the overall themes are shared worldwide, even though names and attributes vary.

We live in a period when the previously rigid sciences have all but lost credibility and suddenly the world, the cosmos, is found to be fluid and scientifically unpredictable. Our ancestors understood that humanity and the land were inseparable aspects of a fluid reality, and developed initiatory or inceptive techniques to bring us into conscious awareness of our holism, extending from land to planet to universe. The environment is both our backyard and the stellar vastness, but intimate understanding begins at home, in the heart of the land.

In previous generations, our questions and answers as to who and why would have taken the form of traditional practices, ancestral lore and wisdom teachings, and no intellectual summary would have been available. Much of this book is a restatement of such lore for contemporary use, but it focuses directly upon the methods and transformative effects of the lore rather than its traditional vehicles of story, song, ritual drama or dance. What we are trying to clarify is the essence of the Underworld traditions, particularly at the deeper transformative levels. These are not outmoded folklore or superstition but living power traditions. The contacts that we make are with living beings and the awakenings are powerful changes of awareness and of vital energy.

Before we discuss 'who' any further, let us consider 'why'. Motive is central to all spiritual arts and disciplines and some of the more powerful spiritual awakenings are dependent upon motive rather than technique. Ideally, the two work in harmony.

Underworld traditions involve entering into a realm of potential, *a realm within the body of the land and planet*. Classic examples of this are found in the faery tradition of the Northern hemisphere, with parallels worldwide. The Underworld, with its realms defined by enduring traditions, visions and inner or spiritual experiences, is the source, the primal image, the wellspring of our own world. This teaching, long ignored or suppressed, has suddenly become intensely relevant for us. It is about the sanctity and power of the planet, approached through human beings building new relationships with their land and fellow inhabitants.

These relationships are empowered by our imagination and have been given form for thousands of years in the suppressed but still active and valid traditions of the Underworld. If we want reasons *why*, they are found in two closely interacting themes. The first is personal and individual or transpersonal change, for the power within the land enables change. The second is environmental, in which we seek a better relationship with the land and come to realize that both land and planet are conscious, and that our own life and consciousness are interwoven within them.

So if you are content with yourself and with the current relationship between humanity and the planet, or with your own relationship to the environment, to your own place, then this book is not for you. If your intuition suggests that humans and land may interact, then the Underworld tradition offers an ancient and potent way towards such interaction.

We have come to one of the spiralling thresholds of human awareness, one of those crossing places that brings us into a new age, not out of nothing but as an octave or rebirth of the seemingly lost ancestral past. This is more simply expressed by saying that our contemporary last-ditch environmental awareness is a recovery of that sense of the sacred land that permeated the lives of our ancestors. And that brings us to the question of *who* we contact, for one of the key experiences of the Underworld is a sharing of ancestral memories and awareness, of jumping across the delusion of rigid linear history to gain a fusion between past and present. This also means, inevitably, fusion between present and future, for once the linear delusion is cleared away we are liberated from the tyranny of cause and effect. This is not escapism but an understanding that our awareness and the inherent power within the land enhance and shape one another.

This enhancement and shaping affect who we contact through our inner work, and how the contact appears to us. Like all perennial spiritual traditions, the Underworld tradition describes interleaved worlds inhabited by many beings. These beings have forms and functions defined for us by tradition, and we are ourselves one such form. The element of *why* is one of spiritual impetus and responsibility, while the element of *who* includes every living being that is aware of the tradition and consciously taking part in it. The contacts are ancestors, teachers, allies and, most powerful of all, those beings called 'sleepers'. They might also be called 'awakeners' but in myth, legend and magical or folklore, emphasis is given first to their sleeping.

A detailed description of the connections between stages of individual transformation and the various orders of being in the Underworld is found on page 125 but we can summarize it as follows, bearing in mind that the questions of why we should follow this path and of who we meet upon it are closely interlinked:

1.   Seeking inner change, you go into the Underworld. This is done through vision (today usually in visualization and meditation), through movement, and in dreams. The entry is often linked to a sacred site or power location, but is not limited to such and can be done anywhere.

2.   Seeking further enlightenment or clarification, you find two closely connected realms of experience. These are the realm of ancestral memory and the realm of non-human companions and allies. In the Northern hemisphere these allies are often from the faery races, found in various forms worldwide. Other orders of life may also be our allies, including animals

and birds, and work with spiritual or magical creatures forms a major branch of the tradition.

3. After experiencing transformations in the Underworld, learning from ancestral memory and forming alliances with other beings, you become aware of deeper levels of consciousness/energy. These are where we meet the 'hidden orders' and the 'sleepers'. The sleepers are found in world myth and religion, while the hidden orders, which are specialized groups or families, are a feature of all esoteric and initiatory lore.

4. Working with your contacts, you seek to awaken the sleepers. This has a catalysing effect upon the land, the planet and all the beings that you share the living world with.

This is the shortest possible summary of how the tradition works, of why we might seek to take part, and of who we work with. The rest of this book expands upon these venerable themes and develops the traditional techniques for modern use.

At this early stage of outlining the who, why and how of Power within the Land, please remember that this is not a psychological or therapeutic process in the materialist or modern sense. Although the perennial wisdom traditions all have detailed models of the psyche, varying from culture to culture but with many points of correspondence, they do not reduce all events to a psychic role. In other words, the beings that you will meet are real, even if our traditional images of them are compromises or convenient interfaces. The Underworld techniques can have a strong effect upon the illusory personality, and utilize energies that arise from the harmonization of people, places and powers. Emphasis upon individual therapy is slight, for like all initiatory traditions healing comes through emergence into a new context, a transformed world, rather than through rationalization and analysis of personal problems.

That transformed world co-exists with our contemporary world, and the potential of changing our collective and individual reality arises constantly. By entering into the Underworld, the source of what we experience as life, death and regeneration through time, we trigger the changes consciously. When we do so, we meet and work with others who share that transformed awareness.

Foreword

The material in this book is drawn from direct experience and aims to communicate ways into such experience to anyone who wishes to share it. The experience is, firstly, my own and that of people who have worked with me or with the Underworld Initiation, and in this sense it is a modern set of experiences described for contemporary use. But within this emphasis upon contemporary practice is the living voice of a great and enduring spiritual tradition, now re-emerging after a period of withdrawal and suppression. During that time the tradition has changed in several ways and there is no claim here to 'authority' which is, essentially, a suppressive factor, both in our seeking and acceptance. What I propose is that you try the practical work for yourself, and you will experience the tradition for yourself.

The book is united out of three elements: in Part 1, specific discussion and exposition with basic exercises; in Part 2, detailed and advanced exercises; and in the third part of the book, a series of appendices. Several of the chapters and appendices include descriptions of some of my own Underworld experiences. These descriptions are related to the ideas discussed in Part 1 and demonstrate how they have worked for me and for others. Some examples draw from group work over the last ten years or so, during which many aspects of the Underworld and Earth Light traditions have opened out, surfaced, regenerated.

One unique element of this book is a set of extracts from direct contact with Underworld beings, usually those who teach the tradition. This *mediation* of lore and practical training has contributed to some of my previous books, but as *Power within the Land* is about 'hidden orders and temples' (terms which we will come to in Chapter 1), it seems appropriate to publish some of the material from such sources in a relatively raw and unedited form. These extracts are either printed in italics with their source listed afterwards or, if they are substantial chunks of text, are introduced individually.

The faery realm was the main subject of *Earth Light*, but this second book focuses upon the deeper levels of the Underworld. Much of Part 1 is drawn from the contacts that may be made in the Underworld, where altered states of consciousness bring interaction and communication with orders of life that are normally withdrawn from us. This withdrawal has not always been the case and there are ample descriptions of the inhabitants of the Underworld in the writings of the pagan and early Christian cultures, plus the immense testimony of folklore.

No space is wasted in arguments proving the existence of such beings, though some discussion of their types and functions is offered as this is essential for the modern reader who might be baffled by the rich variety of traditional lore. There is no quota of belief in the Underworld that needs to be added; it is all direct experience. Of the many groups that I have worked with, no one has entered the Underworld and remained unchanged, and this transformative process is the true result of any initiation.

The exercises, which are by far the most important part of the book, mainly use traditional images and archetypes. Such forms often appear in unusual ways in the Underworld, so the imagery of the visualizations is partly drawn from the core of the tradition and its variants and partly from what I and others have seen. Some of the exercises are, like the teachings of Part 1, drawn from direct Underworld contact. In all cases the writing, structure and presentation are my own, and I have not hesitated to simplify or even completely rework material received from Underworld sources. Exceptions to this reworking are indicated, as described above.

. The creative and discretionary reworking applies particularly to educational material which I was given years ago and did not, at that time, grasp fully. For this book I have reassessed a lot of material that might have been reported verbatim, as I am not a believer in the inherent sanctity of received teachings. Indeed, one of the central requirements of the Underworld tradition is that we challenge all contacts, advice, all suggestions and instructions offered by the beings that we meet. This theme is found in folklore, faery tales and magical ballads, and in the stylized and complex Grail legends which embody the fusion of pagan Underworld lore and Christian mysticism.

While on the subject of contacts and challenges, we need to use common sense. If we meet someone and he or she begins to offer advice or instruction, we assess the situation before we accept . . . and this is, or should be, no different when it comes to spiritual encounters. So do not accept what I have written in any part of this book as if it is some kind of ponderous dogma, but test everything for yourself; when you meet with the beings of the Underworld and faery realm, be prepared for challenges, and prefer arguments to mild acceptance. This important subject of contact, challenge and the trust that is shared afterwards is discussed in various chapters, and can be experienced through practical work with the exercises in this book and in *Earth Light*.

Even the exercises are only openings, beginnings, designed for the compromise of the printed page. They are there to get you started, not to restrict you. The Underworld tradition is an oral one, and there is much that cannot be put into print because of the limitations of the written word. In practice, the visualizations are never the same twice and eventually we learn to work without a script.

Visualization as such is a relatively modern way of working and is suitable for regenerating our often weak inner abilities. Other more physical exercises are also included, particularly those taught through direct contact with Underworld sources. I would recommend that you work with the basic imaginative and visualizing exercises before trying those others, just as you would in any specialist craft or skill that requires preliminary fitness training to reach entry level.

SOURCES OF THE UNDERWORLD TRADITION

The tradition of the Underworld is found worldwide, though different cultures will present it in different forms. Essentially it tells us that truth and transformation are found through entering into a conscious relationship with the land and then with the planet. The rest, which is immense, is the content, methods, adventures and members of the Mystery. I use the word 'Mystery' because Underworld traditions are initiatory, but do not use it in the limited historical sense of referring to a specific mystery cult.

The lore of the Underworld as we find it today, and as it is presented in this book, comes from various sources. In its protean and, to the modern mind, often confused and difficult mass of material, there is great wealth. I have presented some of the Underworld teaching and experiences in my own words and with my own interpretations for contemporary use. In this second volume I have also shown for the first time how the practical exercises are adapted from a core set of teachings, and included some examples of such teachings.

Sources and evidence include, in literary and historical terms, the remnants of religion and magic from the pagan classical world of Greece and Rome (with its far-reaching cultural connections towards Egypt and the East and, according to various ancient sources such as Plato, to Atlantis and the West). Major streams of Underworld lore are found in Celtic pagan tradition, Norse and Germanic pagan sources, and a wide range of poetic, magical, mystical and obscure texts.

To these extensive but obscure and heavily edited literary sources we must add the collective oral traditions, the folklore, tales, songs and ceremonies that involve the Underworld, faery beings, and much that is loosely termed 'shamanic' in popular revivals of paganism today. These are vital sources, vital in the sense of being alive and still part of people's lives, though rapidly diminishing with every generation.

After these historical and collective sources, and only after, we can add *inner contact*, material received and experienced through bringing the tradition alive. I say only after considering the historic and collective sources as a safeguard, and not as any kind of dogma or false scholarship. The collective oral traditions in particular can help modern people, ground us within an ancestral tradition that gives us guidelines, images and a sense of relationship. The older pagan sources offer us the images, mythology and spiritual techniques that were suppressed and corrupted by political Christianity, though not by primal Christianity which was itself suppressed. One of the main reasons for such suppression was to cut people off from all spiritual contacts other than those of state religion. Inner contact, as it is often called today, is the major theme of this book.

From the historical and collective sources, to which we might add early and Celtic Christianity and, by comparison, Gnostic teachings concerning Christ, Lucifer and the Underworld, we gain a body of reference material. They all help us to gain an idea of the Underworld tradition at the foundation of all religion and magic, and how it was gradually suppressed, along with all formal religions of the ancient world, in favour of spiritual totalitarianism. That totalitarianism has now ceased but has left us with a terrible legacy of isolation and antagonism, and the manifest inheritance of materialist abuse and destruction of the planet.

The Underworld tradition itself has historic roots in the most distant past, and much of it seems to come from the megalithic civilization of the Northern hemisphere. But as soon as we say this we have jumped from historic and collective evidence to archaeology combined with intuition and received teachings. Please note that I do not say speculation, for the archaeological evidence alone for an extensive Goddess worship and ancestral reverence, both essential aspects of Underworld lore, is well established.

The living tradition, however, is not a revival based on romantic interpretations of the past. If we work with the Underworld experiences, using methods such as those described in *Earth Light* and in the later chapters of this book, it is possible to activate profound changes of consciousness. One result of these changes is contact with other orders of life, usually invisible or inaccessible to us, but well known to our ancestors. These are not the so-called spirit guides of the Victorian era or the cosy little fairies of fiction. (The spelling *faery* has been used in both volumes when discussing the beings known to our ancestors, with *fairy* referring to whimsical or fantastical fiction.)

Our contacts in the Underworld may have much in common with the perennial teachings of spiritual beings handed down to us from the ancient world, but with the firm distinction that they are contacted through Power within the Land and not through seeking 'higher planes'. This is a very significant difference, for it comes from a tradition in which the land and planet are alive and sacred. Spiritual truth and transformation are found by passing into the land, into the Underworld that leads to the revelation of Earth Light.

This profound tradition runs counter to much that we assume

today in our current spiritual revival, and, of course, to the general assumption that fleeing the world towards light and elevation are the sole hallmarks of spirituality in general. Now that we are beginning to realize that our contempt for our land and planet is leading to our own destruction, we begin to attend to what are coyly called 'environmental issues'. No spiritual tradition is more apt for us now than our oldest, deepest and most neglected one, that of the Underworld.

This is not a tradition for the faint-hearted, fashionable or insincere seeker. The hidden orders of beings and their locations (called 'temples' as they are focusing locations for spiritual powers) are not cuddly and comforting. They will not take our responsibilities away from us.

BECOMING

There is no complete or authoritative version of any of the visions, mythic patterns or empowering narratives handed down within the Underworld and Earth Light or faery traditions. Nor do I make any claim that this book restores and defines such lore. No one can do this, and anyone claiming to have done so is deluded. This vagueness, and the bewildering variety of alternatives in folklore relating to the Underworld, is understandably frustrating to the student or explorer seeking facts and solid ground but it openly hides a powerful truth. The truth is this: spiritual traditions of any sort are always open-ended, and if something has no such open quality it is already defunct.

We see this historically in the dogmatic religions, where an increasing authority and rigidity, for whatever reason, causes spiritual impetus to explode in new forms. In the Christian religion we have the Protestant revolutions as obvious examples, though others may also be discovered as soon as the principle is understood. This is not simply a political or sociological truth, but a spiritual law or pattern. It applies as strongly in one person as it does in an entire civilization, and is shown in the Tarot as the trump of the Blasted Tower. Form that is too rigid, too complete and isolated, can only be broken down, as it leaves no other path for transformation. Underworld work, particularly the primary initiation, is often about breaking before building.

The land, planet and inhabitants are all in a state of *becoming*. There is no grand plan, no all-male universal architect with rigid forms and ultimate control; there is only becoming. If we truly understand this and so become becoming, all limits are removed from us. But remember that the limits, the so-called laws, are what give us identity on any level, in any world. Remove the patterns of temporary limitation and you find death, be it the small death of sleep, the greater death of a phase within one life, or physical death. The Dark Goddess is a death goddess, the destroyer that brings life. She is known as the Weaver of Two Looms, and this is expressed powerfully in the poem *Orchil* by William Sharp, at the beginning of this book.

The process of becoming is found in the non-completion and open-ended nature of oral wisdom teachings, be they folklore or inner teachings. This does not mean that such wisdom is woolly or inept; quite the opposite. Minute, crystal clear and potent images and methods of working abound, but they will never resolve into some grand and complete religion or dogma. Furthermore, the inner aspects of Underworld experience are often surprisingly different from the surface lore that we use to pass within, yet without the diffuse and obscure surface tradition we would have no starting places, no *initiation*. So even the traditional lore unravels itself and becomes something else, for the two looms of the Weaver work simultaneously in the Becoming.

Part 1

Theory and Practice

Introduction

Earth Light explored the transformative potential of the Underworld and faery realm. Ways of achieving the Underworld experience were set out in a simple direct form, with emphasis upon the effects of empowered contact with the faery realm. In this book we will explore deeper levels of the Underworld, and carry the practical work further.

Power within the Land uses techniques that can, with practice and intent, bring us towards a planetary consciousness. This idea of planetary consciousness is much discussed, promoted (even sold), but little understood, and seldom realized within ourselves. Although we are attracted by the idea, we are often unwilling to go through the personal changes that such awareness demands; the Underworld is not an 'as-easy-as' tradition. I hope to have clarified and simplified the language and methods of working as much as possible for contemporary use, but I have not diluted the tradition itself, nor have I held back anything that might be effective for the way ahead.

The basic proposal of this book is that there is an individual power within each land, a power which varies from zone to zone, place to place, but which leads and attunes us to the potent awareness of the planet as a whole being. This could be defined through analogy to the cells of our body, their relationship to our larger body – from entities or parts to the whole human being. But just as the human is not confined or defined by the sum of the parts, neither is the planet. So we might think of ourselves as cells, our lands and planetary zones as organs, and the planet as the whole being. All such beings, people, places, planet, are conscious. In this book, as in the tradition from which it comes, the planet is not passive.

The Underworld and Earth Light tradition works mainly with the consciousness and subtle energies of this planetary being, and shows how these are reflected through human and other life forms. Thus it is different from those teachings or traditions in which the land and its inherent living energies are ignored or rejected.

There are a number of primal or ethnic wisdom traditions worldwide involving the Underworld and its inhabitants; our interaction with the places and people found in the Underworld is vital for our own spiritual growth. Only in recent times, however, has the idea of planetary consciousness been openly attractive to large numbers of people. The ethnic Underworld traditions undoubtedly led to planetary and stellar visions through their radical methods of altering awareness; but they were and are limited to a small number of people, usually dedicated and determined individuals. This is the basis of the idea of initiation which is so often confused with elitism and greed for selfish power. The initiates were often willing to sacrifice self-interest for collective benefit, an idea that permeates the ancestral religions in the system of sacred kingship and which culminated with the sacrifice of Christ.

The mythic truth of Christ is not connected to political religion, and we will explore themes and powers of redemption, sacrifice and resurrection through the Underworld in several ways in this book. Some of the words of the previous sentence may have uncomfortable suppressive connotations for many readers, due to misuse and propaganda in orthodox religious conditioning. This is an unorthodox book, based on perennial spiritual foundations; there is no hidden agenda or attempt to promote any single religion. Primal Christianity was not in conflict with the spiritual impetus of paganism, and we will explore some aspects of the Underworld traditions which they share to the present day. By explore I mean not just a written discussion but an actual set of experiences which are open to anyone working with the methods and examples offered.

With a growing public awareness of the idea of planetary holism and the potential of planetary consciousness, it is time to open out the old traditions and give them a new form. Much of this book is concerned with such opening. An accelerated awareness has already begun to manifest in a most material form: our global computing and communication technology. This means of materializing and exchanging information is still in its most helpless infancy, yet we can detect some of its staggering potential. Such materialization is one of the outer forms of that inner transformation experienced by the seers, magicians and initiates among our ancestors. Even its basic medium, the quartz crystal, has moved from acting as an interface for awareness and subtle energies (past) to working massively with electronic and magnetic data systems (present).

Our global communication technology also hastens the collapse of boundaries and social structures that began to crumble in the early twentieth century. Along with this acceleration of communication technology comes a flurry of renewed interest in spiritual growth and the rapid collapse of dogmatic materialism. This interest is most apparent in the affluent technological societies, the producers of the new technology, at the very heart of the culture in danger of self-destruction. Somehow the idea of planetary awareness seeds itself in Europe, America and Australia; we shall explore the possible origins and effects of this idea, once the 'secret' of the Underworld, throughout this book. More important, we shall seek the impetus behind the idea. This resonates from a specific source within the Underworld, a source that may be approached and contacted by the methods described in our later chapters.

The less technically exploitive countries, those of the so-called Third World, retain their ethnic and regional spiritual and magical arts and traditions. Most of their people are too involved in the struggle for bare survival to think of planetary awareness as a new and exciting idea, yet it has always been accessible through the primal magical arts.

With the immense wealth and technological resources that we already possess but refuse to share, Western and Westernized societies could work towards a united planet. But first there has to be the will, the true intent. This intent begins with you and me as individuals, and may be realized (made real and eventually manifested) in countless different ways. The Underworld and Earth Light traditions and techniques work first upon the individual, bringing transformation and empowerment. If enough individuals undergo such changes, the effect permeates to a collective level, and eventually is reborn in the consciousness of many. You may judge for yourself how effective are the Underworld techniques by trying the exercises and work programmes in this book and in *Earth Light*.

The personal and transpersonal changes through the Underworld Initiation are rapid, but there are also slow changes, long cycles of change that occur within the lands and zones of the planet. These are, in turn, resonances of planetary changes which manifest as collective transformations in human and other life forms. Just as the human body has awareness, modes of consciousness that interact with the 'parts' of its holism, so does the planet.

We have limited materialist models of such changes, often self-contradictory or prejudiced. Our scientific reconstructions of past ages and their life forms are examples of models of long cycles of change, drawn from selective preconditioned evidence and full of retrospective assumptions. They define a historical world that never really existed. This situation is discussed by Owen Barfield in his book *Saving the Appearances*.[1]

What is valuable is not the relative validity of materialist or esoteric models or world views but the idea of cycles of change, of a fluid or protean world *which transforms itself*. The various models are, in themselves, a tiny part of the transformative process.

If there is truly a major change of planetary consciousness happening right now, we are part of it. We may think of ourselves as victims of history, carried upon the waves of change, or we may feel that we have a more grandiose part to play. The Underworld traditions propose that vast time scales and tides of change may be understood only within altered states of consciousness. This is why the Underworld is associated with both prophetic and ancestral knowledge. The alterations are not made through raising consciousness in the accepted sense through prayer or meditation but through passing into the body and power of the land. This attuning does not bring a passive vegetative state or a lowering of awareness and energy, but a dynamic energizing and enlightenment. The power within the land resonates to the power of the planetary being. So may we come to planetary consciousness.

The understanding that comes is not a type of superknowledge but a grounding within rhythms, visions, modes and streams of consciousness that do not involve serial knowledge or linear explanation. The awareness works from under the conditioned thresholds, not in the divisive sense of the

'unconscious' of psychotherapy but from realms of consciousness which are our lost home as planetary beings. And this is
the shortest way to that enlightenment which so many cannot
find through techniques of raising energy and consciousness.
Our attempt to elevate our consciousness/energy towards enlightenment or divinity above is similar to the linear, divisive
antagonistic idea of the 'conquest of space'. It is a long, long
way to the stars 'out there', yet the Earth is of the Universe and
we are already home!

REGENERATION

The land, which means any land, region or country, has regenerative power. This power within the land is drawn from
the planet, accordinging to zones, seasons and stellar relationships. This is not a new theory and has been represented in
many different ways for millennia. Indeed, each culture, each
century, produces its own way of describing the power within
the land. It may be as myth or as materialist science. Just as we
are discovering that materialist sciences are wilfully blind to the
living earth, so we must remember that our ancestors dwelt
almost entirely in the mythic or dream dimensions, living a life
more collective than individual. Neither state of consciousness
is suitable for us now . . . we are moving into something other.

This book explores some of the possibilities of regeneration
through power within the land, for both ourselves and the
planet. It uses the language of the perennial wisdom traditions,
but in a simple and direct way. This is not a book on 'occultism',
which is a nineteenth century invention, now, like most Victorian
engines, virtually derelict and obsolete. It is instead an exploration of reality apprehended through meditation, visualization
and our individual and collective energies. You are invited to
test the power of the techniques and traditions described in this
book . . . to explore the power within the land for yourself.

There is a simple inward-moving order of relationship in
such potential: humans; land; planet. This is mirrored in the
outward-looking pattern of Moon, Sun and stars, which
formed the Three Worlds of relativity in the perennial wisdom
traditions. Humans for the Lunar World, which is everything
encompassed by the orbit of the Moon, everything of the Earth
and the sublunar sphere of energy and awareness. The land for

the Solar World with its rhythm of planetary orbits causing day and night, summer and winter, light and dark. The planet for the Stellar World or stars ... which are found again deep within the Underworld beyond the light of Moon or Sun.

The simple pattern described is not an obscure mystical insight but a statement of our relationship, collective and individual, to our total environment. The Moon, Sun and stars are three relative spheres of awareness, as well as, in scientific terms, relative conditions or patterns of matter and energy. As the energy of the stars reaches our planet, it is modified first by that of the Sun and its solar system, then by that of the Moon. Stars, Sun, Moon ... Planet, Land, Humans. That is our relative situation both as science and the perennial wisdom traditions perceive it.

Stars: Planetary matter and energy, universal being.
Sun: Land and seas, under solar and solar system influence.
Moon: Human (and other orders of life within the Lunar World).

There is a mirroring within this simple model (see Figure 1) for the stellar state, the furthest out from us in a linear sense, is

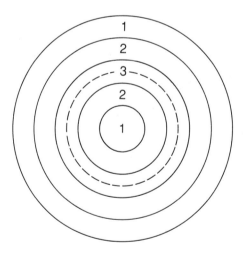

1 = STELLAR WORLD/PLANET EARTH

2 = SOLAR WORLD/LANDS + SEAS

3 = LUNAR WORLD/LIFE FORMS

Figure 1 The Three Realms of Being

also the substance *within* the body of the planet; *emerging* as the surface are the lands and seas, while *upon* the surface of the land are the various orders of life.

This reflection is found again in our modes and levels of consciousness: our surface habitual mode is usually upon the Lunar and Earth level; our inner life accessed through meditation or other changes of direction and intent is upon the Solar level; while our deepest mode accessed through contemplation or revelation is universal and Stellar.

THE PLASTIC MIND, MIRROR OR SHIELD

The planetary mind is *plastic* in the true sense of the word. Our contemporary meaning, of moulded goods made from various substances, demonstrates a profound truth. The word 'plastic' comes from the Greek verb *plasso*, which means 'to form'. Popular use identifies plastic with a range of end-products and their materials, but the word means *having the power to give form*, and *capable of change*. The planet has the power to give form and without this power you would not be reading this book, I would not be writing it, for we would not exist as planetary beings.

This may seem a simplistic truth but it is the key to some remarkable insights. In the perennial wisdom traditions, our bodies are the most potent form of spiritual realization; through the Underworld and Earth Light arts and disciplines we become aware of the relationship between ourselves and the planet. We intentionally seek ways in which the planetary power will transform us. Those ways are well known and accessible, but currently neglected.

A great truth is mirrored in ourselves, the relationship between form and mind. There is no inanimate object, no separate observer and observed. This truth has always been known to us and was widespread in the ancient Elemental world-view. We will return to the idea of the Elements in later chapters.

Underworld lore is about transformation and regeneration, two closely related processes which are of the Earth, and earthy. Without the Earth-form there is nothing to transform; without the Earth-mind there is no power of transformation. We find this amply demonstrated in the Christian myth, for even in the heavily edited orthodox Gospels, Jesus enters the Underworld (a myth known as 'the Harrowing of Hell', which we will return to in Appendix 3). Within his ancestral rock chamber, the tomb belonging to his uncle Joseph, Jesus is transformed. Only after his plunge into the transformative earth does Jesus ascend as a resurrected spiritual being.

This myth originally indicated the fusion of the Christian revelation with those of the pagan sacrificial cults. On another level it concerns the relationship between the great spiritual beings known to us as Christ and Lucifer, the Anointed and the Shining One. We shall return to this theme in Chapter 6, where we will bypass suppressive propaganda and examine the myth of Lucifer afresh in a modern context. For the moment it is enough to suggest that this myth describes phases in the harmonic interaction between the Earth and the Sun and stars, bearing in mind that these are all living beings with vast patterns and cycles of consciousness/energy.

If we attune to our planetary cycles, we choose participation and awareness. Our intent or will is a catalysing factor, and can cause rapid personal change through the Underworld. This intentional change has always been the aim of initiation but in recent years there has been a rapid collective change and the initiatory arts are moving into a new and more open phase. Within this wide change we find a lot of ephemeral New Age nonsense, but this is essentially froth bubbling away. Once the transformation has settled, we shall discover its essence.

Our planet is composed of all four Elements, but the Element of Earth is the plastic changeable matter that gives it form out of the intent of the planetary mind. At dedicated sacred sites or at natural power sites, the power of the Elements takes specific patterns. In some locations this is due to input from human and other beings, while in other locations patterning of energy is through an organ of the planetary body. The most potent power sites are those where the human and planetary consciousness/energy are intentionally merged. Such power sites may be created afresh by the methods of the Underworld tradition, and are enabled by the hidden orders and temples in concert with human and other beings.

1. The Hidden Orders and Temples

WHAT ARE THE HIDDEN ORDERS AND TEMPLES?

There are several arts or categories within the esoteric and spiritual disciplines worldwide. The Western and Northern traditions are immensely rich in such lore, encompassing the profound wisdom of the classical civilizations, Celtic and Norse magical religions, and the widespread shamanistic practices found throughout Europe and North America. To these we may add the pyramid building civilizations of Egypt and South America, which are linked in esoteric teaching traditions to Atlantis. Much of the religion and magic in Europe derives from the megalithic culture which predates all of the others. At the foundation of all religion, magical arts and spiritual disciplines is the lore of the Underworld.

The various arts include elemental and energy work, changing modes of consciousness, and contact and interaction with other orders of life, especially those within the metaphysical or non-material dimensions. In practice, the three arts interlink and are united through work with the physical body, which is one of the most neglected and suppressed traditions in the West.

In this chapter, and throughout this book, we will concentrate on the art of *contact* in the Underworld tradition. As we discussed and experienced in *Earth Light*, contact and interaction with the faery races bring powerful changes of awareness and energy. The same can be said of work with spiritual animals, and one of the lost 'secrets' of Underworld lore was and is the threefold cooperation of human, faery and animal co-walkers. This is described in Chapter 6 and is then brought into our practical work, entering the deeper levels of the Underworld.

Our contact with beings in the deeper Underworld is usually made after the experience of the faery realm, and at this stage we should examine the theory and practice of contact before defining those deeper levels and contacts. This short summary is important, not in the sense of trying to prove the validity of contact (you can try this and prove it for yourself using the exercises), but to highlight the difference between the Underworld tradition of contact and others.

Teachings and practices involving contact are not as strange and obscure as we might think, for they simply involve *interaction* between humans and other orders of life. As this occurs constantly in all aspects of our existence, the idea of magical or metaphysical contact should be seen as an extension of something which we already do, and the same rules of common sense that we use in daily life should apply. Indeed, most magical laws, far from being obscure, complex and grandiose, are harmonics of that which we know already, though often they are the originals and our regular knowledge derives from them.

In orthodox religion (especially in the corrupt monotheistic cults which have recently dominated the Western psyche but are now in a state of collapse), spiritual contact is severely limited. On the positive side this limitation may lead to a true religion or mysticism of unity, in which all that is, all being, is known to be Divine. On the negative side (the most prevalent), the limitation of spiritual contact leads to antagonistic dualism, to psychic and spiritual isolation, to hostility to the natural world and, inevitably, to ruthless materialism. Our contemporary antagonistic materialism is the direct product of monosexual religion.

The monotheistic monosexual deity is exclusive, in the sense that he excludes, is removed and distant from us, in the sense that he is found 'in heaven', and is stereotypically male. This unhealthy nonsense was promulgated by force of arms as a state religion and deeply sown into the Western psyche by long-term programmes of manipulation and suppression. It has very little to do with the original spiritual reality of Christ. But 2000 years is a short time in comparison with the life of the inherent Goddess religion of our culture, which has never been truly suppressed. Underground religions are of the

Underworld, where the Goddess rules over all cults of gods and goddesses, arts and sciences. Our primal Goddess religion is inclusive, for nothing is excluded, inferior or cast out, and such a religion involves many spiritual contacts.

Some variants of Christianity are, of course, grafted onto the roots of paganism and allow contact with spiritual beings, such as the saints, the Trinity, the Virgin, and angels and archangels. These structures are uneasy compromises between the metaphysics of paganism, popular tradition, and a constantly shifting orthodox dogma.

In many Eastern religions a host of interrelated beings are worshipped and contacted. Here too we find state religions grafted onto older roots, but often in a more harmonious manner. One of the romantic attractions of Eastern religions for Westerners is the rich variety of contacts, of deities, of realities suppressed by Christianity. Thus they can satisfy a true spiritual need for such contact, the same need that is found in nineteenth-century spiritualism and twentieth-century channelling.

The need for contact is far more than either ignorance or loneliness, which materialistic Westerners often assume are at the foundation of such beliefs and practices. Rather than rationalize our urge for spiritual contact and 'explain' it, the Underworld tradition suggests that it is something that we *are* and that the contacts *are already* part of our true life, our true condition or reality from which we have temporarily excluded ourselves. This does not mean that the beings found in the Underworld (or any spiritual tradition) are all aspects or fragments of the human psyche . . . it means quite the opposite. The human being is an aspect or fragmented moment of a life-continuum, of a holism. Thus when we seek contacts, as in the magical and spiritual arts, we are acknowledging our true selves which are interactive rather than static and isolated.

Before the political monotheism of the Western cultures gained its stranglehold, our inherent religion was (and is) both pantheistic and polytheistic. It is not at all certain that the word 'worship' applies to the religious attitudes and practices of our ancestors, as their 'religion' was inseparable from living. Within and including all other beings was and is the Goddess, the Great Mother of the Worlds, the Universe. She simultaneously creates and destroys. In the Underworld tradition, she is frequently known as the Weaver Goddess. All beings are interconnected by her weaving.

Our contemporary revival of witchcraft and paganism demonstrates not only the collapse of Christianity but our deep need for forms and images that bring living contact, a realization of connection. We no longer need to seek this in the religions of the East as our own ancestral lore is suddenly reappearing. It is in this way that our world's cultures meet and know one another spiritually, through a balanced interaction of what is true for East and West, North and South. This approach to planetary unity through the Underworld forms part of the received teaching in Chapter 6.

There is no suggestion here that we must go 'back to nature', for romanticism plays no part in the Underworld traditions. Once we have entered the Underworld, we find that the nature to which we idealistically sought to return is protean, taking many adaptable forms. Much of the work of the hidden orders and contacts in the deeper realms involves profound collective and planetary changes, just as the Underworld Initiation involves individual transformation. Within this flow of shapes and changes there are some enduring matrices or archetypes, but even these change.

The faery realm is the original pristine world, the nature from which our natural world is devolved, but if we seek to fix our world in some ideal mould, we poison it. This may be the ideal mould of scientific manipulation, or the ideal of the utterly natural and unadjusted. We need contact with the faery realm to adjust our current imbalances but we cannot return our outer realm, our consensual world, to that first image. Indeed, the faery realm itself devolves from an originative image which has never been, but the varied patterns and interaction of the worlds, dimensions, realities, conditions, are aspects of that image coming into being. Through changes of awareness, through widening and deepening contact, we come closer to this truth of Being which causes the realms, the worlds, to live and interact.

The faery realm and its inhabitants are the nearest to our own and Underworld transformation often begins with this type of contact, though it may sometimes be bypassed altogether. The enduring survivals of faery lore and living contact were widespread in Europe until the early years of this century, and in many of the less urban regions still survive in an attenuated form. These are the root traditions of contact with non-material beings, the allies, co-walkers, helpers and companions of our ancestors, Very little of this immense tradition has appeared in modern paganism, though it is sometimes found in the popular revival of shamanism as a spiritual alternative among urbanites.

Within the Underworld tradition, which involves faery lore combined with the inheritance of paganism from all European cultures, there are specific methods for making contact. Beyond the faery companions and the realms of primal beauty and terror which are often encountered first, there are others. These are the realms of the hidden orders of the Underworld, and some skill and experience is necessary before we can contact them and work with them. There are distinct entities in distinct places, usually reached through changes of awareness combined with physical travel, or through specific physical and imaginative activities and transformations. The Underworld is the mirror of our own, with all acts of significance reversed. A little movement will take you a long way and the vehicle is your own consciousness and energy within that of the land, not an isolated travel machine in conflict with it.

In the deeper Underworld experiences, we are taught that we come to the hidden orders as a team, a partnership of human, faery and spiritual creature. The hidden orders are found in locations, traditionally described as temples, which are sometimes but not inevitably linked to geomantic sites within the land. The Triune Alliance (see Chapter 6) is a balanced relationship between a creature or creatures (popularly known as totem beasts, though this is an inaccurate term), faery allies, and one or more humans. Usually the human works alone to find these companions, and the Underworld tradition places emphasis upon individual work and responsibility rather than group worship or social membership. The apparent isolation of the human in early stages leads, however, to substantial contact in the other realms, though this (like all contact and relationships in any circumstance) should be handled with integrity and discretion.

The Triune Alliance is not essential for entry to the deeper realms of the Underworld, for it is possible to work without it or with only one of the two types of ally, be it animal or faery. Ancestors usually count as humans, though there are significant exceptions to this which are discussed in later chapters. However, most of the practical work in this book assumes that you have established faery and creature allies, and some of the examples of instruction from Underworld contacts are very clear on this subject. The expanded visualization/vision in Chapter 7 combines creature and faery contact before moving further into the Underworld, where powerful companions are encountered. This exercise encapsulates the entire process of the Triune Alliance in a simple manner, but cannot replace long-term individual work.

The hidden contacts are hidden in the obvious sense that we cannot reach them through our habitual or conditioned means of communication, nor are they accessible through the popular types of meditation or through most religious paths or spiritual disciplines. They have to be approached by very specific and carefully attuned methods at first but after the dynamic initiatory stages, they become progressively easier to contact. Some of these orders or Underworld locations are hidden deliberately, and access is only given to a few. This limited access is, however, changing, for some of the hidden orders and temples seem to be opening contact on a wider scale for the first time in many hundreds of years.

As the time-scale in the Underworld is different to our own consensus on time, this is not an easy subject to define in detail, but the opening of contact seems to be due to an impending change in planetary awareness. Such changes manifest or surface through particular places and people initially, then gain a wider collective and planetary momentum. The three key elements to any Mystery are powers, places and people, including creatures and non-human beings that *people* or *populate* any and all places.

If, as is usually the unfortunate case, we isolate ourselves from our broader and deeper life contacts, the surfacing of change can be explosive. This is the truth of Vulcan and Pluto, which can be eruptive Underworld powers that destroy in order to create anew. The deeper levels of Underworld contact enable us to align to changes, even to participate in them consciously. The transformative powers may then be mediated through the various allied orders of life, human, faery, and creatures. This is not as grand or complex as it sounds, for in a confused and imbalanced way it happens continually. The key difference is one of our own conscious intent.

The Underworld Initiation begins with individual sacrifice of the personality, plunging willingly into the hitherto mysterious realms of the land and planet. After many transformations we surface again, able to mediate initiatory powers to both the land and its people.

THE UNDERWORLD AND THE PLANETARY MIND

The Underworld is the mind of the planet. This planetary mind is the totality of all matter, energy and consciousness associated with the planet; it exists upon a planetary time-scale. The planetary cycles are part of a stellar time-scale which encompasses our own relative time, defined by the movements of the solar system.

Just as our own consciousness is not solely defined by the physical brain and body, the planet has an individuality and awareness that may not be defined by material form. Meditation teaches us through direct experience that we may redirect our attention inwardly, the balancing opposite of our customary direction. When we do so we find a reality that is not limited to the materialist biological model, for we do not experience reduction of awareness to a cellular state, but a powerful expansion. The meditative disciplines also enable access to realms of being that are closed to us when our attention and will are outwardly directed. The Underworld and Earth Light experiences, accessible through various means including meditation and visualization, teach us the reality within the land and planet.

This inner reality is as subjective or objective as any other, for all realities are defined and conditioned by the roles and rules of the participants. Particle physics has recently 'discovered', via the hard road of modern science, that there are no observers, only participants. This simple truth has been taught for millenia in the esoteric traditions, though the models (world-models) within which it is expressed vary from culture to culture and from land to land.

The Underworld traditions teach us ways towards conscious participation in the life-patterns of the planet; through the simple but neglected method of passing awareness *downwards* into the land. Popular meditation techniques, regardless of their origin, are inwardly balancing, for through them our attention is drawn away from outward-reaching habits and focused inwardly. Underworld work gives us the essential balance below, drawing attention away from our other addiction or obsession, that of escaping upwards to a distant light.

The obsession with elevation is only a variant of the outward-seeking trap, for both depend upon rejection or dualism. We find this at its most serious in religions and spiritual practices which raise energy/consciousness upward above the head, rejecting (or more arrogantly 'redeeming') all that is below.

In externalized materialism, this old spiritual arrogance appears as humanity's self-acclaimed right to exploit nature. Interestingly it is science today that has realized that dualism and lack of responsibility towards the natural world leads directly to our own destruction; the current spiritual revival still uses, to a great extent, the dualistic Christian-materialist model. Light is always above, while superior masters and angels will intervene to save or at least lecture us through channelled communications. In the Underworld tradition the land and all living beings upon and within it are holy, sacred, and spiritually and physically aspects of one being, of which we are an integral part.

As the planetary patterns of awareness and our individual and collective human life-patterns are aspects of a holism, we may enter into planetary awareness directly for, of course, we are already there.

We need not think of the land and planet as having separate minds in an exclusive sense, as we are conditioned to think of each other, but that our own awareness is of the planet, it *is* the planetary awareness. If, as is often the case, we are unable to make the conscious dive, to plunge directly into a state of planetary being, we should work through the land, that part of the planetary zone upon which we live and to which we are organically attuned.

The Underworld is the mind of the planet and is not limited to the parts that we identify through our self-limited participation. Like our own minds it has many patterns and is protean and (in the true sense of the word) plastic. Although the Underworld Initiation begins at home, as the primal power traditions are always regional and ethnic, it does not stay there. At the present time we are moving out of some of our old racial patterns but not out of the enabling limitation of regions, lands and zones, which are both geomantic and spiritual.

Each relative entity, from zones to microscopic life forms, is a part of the planetary mind. The substance of the world, defined by the Four Elements, is also part of the planetary mind. We are of it, and yet we reject and abuse both the planet and ourselves. The Underworld initiates plunge willingly and deeply into the planetary mind, seeking to pass into it and be changed by it rather than reject it and rise away from it.

THE PARADOX OF EARTH LIGHT

There are some significant links between the Underworld and the more widely popularized idea of rising to the light, or 'rising through the planes'. Initially such links seem to be paradoxical, for the deeper we reach into the Underworld the closer we come to light. In folk tradition, the faery realm is filled with illumination, but there is no sight of the Sun or Moon. The light is that of the sacred land, the primal world, the light of the stellar universe inherent within the body and substance of the planetary being.

In the pagan myths this light was that of the Goddess, and to be at one with her light involved passing through darkness. The best known name for her is Isis, who was both black and white. The Black Isis is simultaneously the depths of the Underworld and the depths of the universe, while the White Isis is the light of the planet and the light of the stars. The Earth Light experiences bridge between the planetary mind (of which we are an integral part) and the stellar consciousness.

There is a widespread assumption in esoteric literature that the Goddess of the Earth and Moon, known as Isis and by countless other names, is a lesser power than, say, the God of the Sun. This idea is merely propaganda or patriarchy. Apart from the Underworld tradition which does away with such hierarchies and propaganda, we need only do a little homework to discover that the Earth, Moon, sun and stars manifested deities of both sexes. In psychic and magical terms, the way in which we approach these entities, regarding them as male, female or androgyne, makes definable changes within ourselves.

Ironically, the patriarchal and prejudiced Victorian scholars of myth and legend identified over a century ago that there were many major examples of solar goddesses and lunar gods in ancient religion, a well-documented body of truth that is virtually ignored in the modern revival of paganism and the New Age movement.

Earth Light is a term that developed from the first book, in which the light of the faery realm is revealed. The idea of the Earth as a world of light was once widespread in religion and magic, though orthodox political Christianity fought constantly to suppress such a liberating truth.

Today we inherit the suppressive propaganda, both in the form of materialism and in many unchallenged assumptions in our spiritual revival and New Age enthusiasm. Much nonsense is attached to the idea of the Earth and Underworld as negative, dark, even corrupt. We must flee, we are told, the drag of matter, or alternatively we must seed the passive Earth with manly light from the higher worlds. This antagonistic sexist propaganda is rehashed in endless ways by people who have never once entered the sacred land in meditation or vision, and found it vibrant and filled with light.

The Christian war waged upon our world has subtly evolved into arrogant abuse through science and industry, but it does not stop there. New spirituality seems determined to find only the higher planes, the Masters, and escape from responsibility. We dread confrontation with any power that will act as a catalyst for true inner change, we fear and reject the Earth by our crass assumption that spiritual Masters, angels or a Saviour will appear in some external manner to save us from ourselves.

The Underworld tradition teaches that we must confront and pass through our fear and rejection of the Earth as a transformative illuminating matrix. Beyond the fearful darkness is Earth Light, found by moving our energy and awareness into the body and power of the land. This light is our closest light, the divine Being in matter or substance, in living interaction with its individual and collective creations. The land and planet are alive, and our spiritual reality derives from this life just as much as our physical reality. Indeed, the Underworld tradition makes little or no distinction between physical and spiritual . . . these are merely clumsy words.

ESTABLISHING UNDERWORLD CONTACTS

The hidden orders tend to be groups or extended families, sisterhoods or brotherhoods. Not all members are human or ex-human (see Glossary), but we tend to work with the ex-humans. These hidden orders have well-defined functions and work programmes: they are specialists, though not in the scientific materialist sense. Their specialization is as much of their inherent qualities and energies as it is of the tasks that they undertake. In the Underworld the life is the work, and being is more effective than doing.

The term 'hidden orders' may sound pompous to modern ears, and has unfortunate connotations of nineteenth century theosophy and the ridiculous stereotypical 'Masters'. The title is a traditional one, handed down orally, and does not imply hierarchy or superiority. The hidden orders are not evangelists seeking converts, nor do they make any claims for steering or saving errant humanity. They usually shun general contact and are, in some ways, out of touch with our own shifting vision of contemporary humanity. This situation is currently changing.

When I first encountered some of these contacts in the late 1970s, I had never worked with the Triune Alliance (see Chapter 6) and had many initial difficulties with my experiences. With hindsight and further instructions in the Underworld tradition, I now know that some of these difficulties were unnecessary and that there were easier ways of working. But each individual coming to the deeper levels of the Underworld has to learn of his or her weaknesses: mine, at that time, were a ruthless determination to do things the hard way and listen to no one. When I learned to listen to the tradition itself and its teachers, many remarkable spiritual techniques were revealed, and some of these are put into a contemporary form in this book.

The whole subject of learning from spiritual contacts is frequently confused and can become obscure when we seek deeper orders of the Underworld: this is one aspect of the term *hidden*, quite different from any idea of elitism or separatism. The hidden orders and temples tend to take form in our imaginations in the guise of past ages, and in some cases they are literally the brotherhoods and sisterhoods, the sacred families, of our ancestral magical religion. But much of the colouration comes from our own personal interpretation and even more from the social ambience of our time.

Sometimes it comes from the social ambience of an intermediary, and my first Underworld contact was a good example of this. He was, ironically when I think of my distaste for such figures, a Victorian or Edwardian occultist, who began to teach in my dreams after my Underworld Initiation (see *Earth Light* for a description of the initiation). This teacher was eventually replaced by other contacts, always moving back in time, which for us is usually a sign of deepening Underworld contacts and awareness. This first teacher of Underworld traditions was determined that I should study extensively, as he was a learned scholar as well as a very experienced magician. Most of the material that I learned from him was in a rather Victorian mould, and this creeps through in parts of my earlier book *The Underworld Initiation*.[2] Once the deeper contacts were established this teacher faded away, though it is possible to recover contact through focusing upon certain key images associated with him.

The older level of Underworld contact with human mentors is often what we loosely call megalithic. In *Tomb of a King* (*Earth Light*, Appendix 6), I describe and quote from one such contact, about as far removed as one can be in time and consciousness from the Victorian era while still being clearly human. The twenty-first century seems to have a resonance, a harmonic connection to the megalithic period, as if turning a spiral brings us into line with it although we are removed from it in a superficially linear time sense (see Figure 2).

In *Earth Light* we looked at some of the implications of imagery and apparent cultural influences in the faery realm. Beings from the faery realm are often clothed in the fashions of our past eras and they tend to draw imagery from our collective storehouse, the one that is preserved in folk tales and ballads. In the case of the hidden orders and temples, this borrowing and malleability is less common. Most of them are ex-human beings, people who now live in the Underworld (see *Earth Light* for a full discussion of this idea in faery tradition), and tend to be coloured only by our own filters of perception, for we will often mould the presentation of a contact unwittingly.

One of the hallmarks of Underworld perception, however, is that these powerful contacts are not susceptible to moulding or wishful thinking, and will assert very firm identities and appearances. This firmness is also found in the faery realm, where contacts will appear to the inner vision in all manner of archaic and outlandish costumes, but cannot be fantasized into something else. In either case it is one of the signs of a true contact rather than a construct of wishful thinking.

Another important feature of the deeper Underworld is *masking*, which is traditionally involved with *challenging*. Powerful

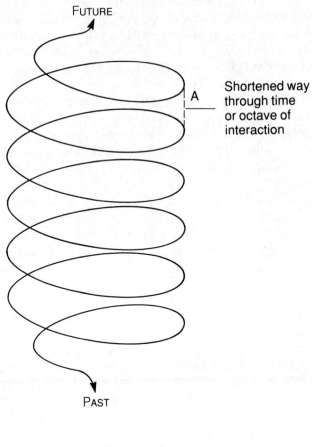

FUTURE

A   Shortened way
through time
or octave of
interaction

PAST

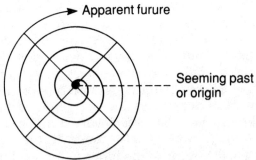

Apparent furure

Seeming past
or origin

Figure 2 The Spiral of Ancestral Time

contacts, allies, co-walkers and companions will first appear in a superficial form. This may be due to our own imaginative restrictions, or, as is often the case, it may be a test. Underworld allies from non-human races frequently try to frighten us and sometimes are used as masks or watchers by ex-human or ancestral contacts. If challenged, a deeper identity or contact is revealed.

Masking and unmasking, testing and challenge are patterns found over and over again in folklore, myth and magical arts. When working with Underworld experiences, always take the tradition literally, for this is how it works. The contacts expect to be challenged, and may question and challenge us in turn. Once the transformation cycle has occurred and the contact is made clear, they will remain steady and may be met with repeatedly. Over a period of time you are likely to move from contact to contact as you yourself transform. Overworld and Underworld are the same in this respect: we do not stay in infant condition or kindergarten for long.

The orders that you are likely to contact through the exercises and methods in this book are as follows (the names are traditional and poetic rather than pompous formal titles, so do not expect to meet humans claiming or offering membership!):

1. The Sisters at the Back of the North Wind
2. The Order of Justified Men
3. The Orders of Prophets and Sybils
4. Sacred Kings and Priestess Queens
5. Personal and ancestral contacts

The fifth category may come out of any of the four main ones, or may be individual and independent. All four orders are described shortly and ways of contacting them are found throughout the practical chapters. Do not expect any of these people to appear in glowing robes or for their temples to be vast pillared halls of grandeur. As a rule only the most trivial inner contacts appear in this manner, usually from traditions which involve the enervating method of 'rising through the planes'. This popular meditational technique can give temporary ecstasies, but is usually combined with isolation from the land while aiming at something 'higher'. There is no state or condition more holy than the Earth, and in the depths of the Earth we may find spiritual enlightenment more truly than by flying upwards. In our myths, the high flyer crash-lands, but whoever finds the Earth Light emerges transformed and regenerated. The complete myth cycle often tells us that the wounded flyer can only be healed in the Underworld.[3]

1.   *The Sisters at the Back of the North Wind*   This order is found at a very deep level of awareness, equating to the depths of the planet. Traditionally they are a group of women, once priestesses of the Great Goddess, but living out of time. They act to bring in profound far-reaching collective changes, changes working upon a planetary scale rather than a localized or individual one. They appear in meditation or to the inner vision as hooded women, often small in size but with a sense of great power and knowledge.

2.   *The Order of Justified Men*   These are a group of men who have become transformed through the initiations of the faery realm. They often appear in meditation or to the inner vision as teachers or guides. Traditionally these are thinkers, seers, poets, bards and others who have sworn service to the faery queen, and at the end of their period of service have chosen to remain in the Underworld. Some returned to the upper human world, and subsequently vanished into the faery realm again instead of undergoing normal ageing and death. In widespread faery traditions of the Northern hemisphere these (ex-human) men play in important role as mentors and protectors of human men and women during faery experiences, particularly at the deeper levels.

3.   *The Orders of Prophets and Sybils*   These are groups of men and women who were once associated with the great prophetic cults and wisdom of the pagan religions. They span across various cultures from the ancient lost civilizations to the historical period, including Greek, Roman, Scandinavian and Celtic. They are found at the levels of awareness that attune us to the prophetic powers of the Dark Goddess.

4.   *Sacred Kings and Priestess Queens*   These contacts often represent a level corresponding to the most ancient cultures, though the practice of sacred kingship and of priestess queens who mediate the Goddess persisted well into historical times in Europe, and is found in attenuated form in the Grail legends from Celtic tradition. Contact with such beings involves a

strong relationship with the sacred land, and with mediation of changes in which the individual acts selflessly for the benefit of many. They are often localized, acting through zones or lands. Despite this localization, or perhaps because of it, the Sacred Kings and Priestess Queens merge the pagan and Christian sacrificial Mysteries in an unbroken line of inheritance.

5. *Personal and Ancestral Contacts*   These are the spiritual contacts that are your own within the Underworld, and will include faery allies and spiritual animals, as well as ancestors and ex-humans. The first four categories are all ex-human, though they often mediate the power of god and goddess forms. The fifth category may come from any of the four main ones, or may be individual and independent. Sometimes we establish Underworld contacts who lead us to deeper levels or, after a period of work, reveal their connection within the hidden orders.

Exceptions to our caution against 'obvious' stereotypes are timeless visions and contacts from our great temple-building civilizations, which often occur in the standard esoteric arts but do not feature strongly in the Underworld. When such locations do appear in an Underworld context they are often seen as the caverns, labyrinths, chambers and tunnels *beneath* the formal temples, the foundations where the power originates. Ostentatious shows of power are matters of human politics rather than spiritual reality. The Underworld reveals immense power, but usually in simple forms.

In the next chapter we will begin practical work that is designed to cause the changes of awareness that bring us into contact with the various beings within the Underworld. We will return to our discussion of communication and contacts again in more detail in Chapters 4 and 5, but before going into this further, some of the basic experiences of the Underworld Initiation should be examined. In Chapter 3 you will find the effects of the Underworld Initiation described, some of which are likely to occur when you begin the programme suggested on page 122, starting with the exercises in Chapter 2.

As the Underworld transformations vary from person to person, there is no rigid or 'complete' sequence of events, but in the following chapters an idealized model is described. Your own experiences will match this in various ways. Some intellectual grasp of the idealized sequence of events resulting from the Underworld Initiation is helpful with our overall theme of the hidden orders and the arts of contact and awakening, but explanations or analyses cannot replace direct experience.

2. Basic Techniques and Exercises

A basic Underworld visualization is the first unit of the work programme (page 29), and you should experience it as soon as possible. At this stage you might prefer simply to read it through as a visionary narrative before moving into it in depth. For those who are not familiar with empowered visualization, a short introduction and set of guidelines is included before the narrative itself.

GUIDELINES FOR EMPOWERED VISUALIZATION

Empowered visualization is an ancient technique for producing both inner and outer transformation which is currently having a widespread revival after centuries of neglect and isolated minority use. The basics are simple but the results are remarkable and far-reaching.

Through a clearly defined story, sometimes called an induction narrative, we are led into a state of consciousness which is, simultaneously, the place or realm of the narrative. This differs from both free association and fantasy in several ways, the most valuable being the traditional imagery. Empowered visualizations are driven, so to speak, by the coherent images, which have been used in some cases for thousands of years without disruption. They lead into specific states of consciousness and have specific effects upon us, both short and long-term. They involve images and experiences of people, places and powers within the tradition that they embody.

The reality or non-reality of the beings and the world

described are not so much a matter of discussion but of experience. They are as real, if not more real, than many contemporary beliefs, world-views, scientific models of existence, habitual or consensual activities, and so forth.

The foundation for this art is in collective lore such as storytelling, narrative and mythic ballads and poems, and ritual drama and dance. Specialized variants were used in the ancient temples, with particular reference to mythic cycles and the images of gods and goddesses inhabiting sacred places. In both mysticism and magic such techniques were highly developed, though suppressed by orthodox religion.

The technique consists of three basic stages:

1.   Sit in silence for a few moments, stilling your sense of time, space and interactions or events.
2.   Following the imagery of the narrative, which should be *heard*, with your eyes closed. You enter into the story and travel through it, returning to your starting point.
3.   On conclusion, sit in silence for a few moments and reorientate yourself and, if preferred, make notes.

If this method is new to you it may take a few repetitions to restimulate your visionary ability: for most of us, years of television watching have caused our inner vision to atrophy. The inner vision gradually comes alive and the images of the narrative take on a clarity and energy of their own.

If you are working in a group, take it in turns to be the reader while the others enter into the vision. If you are working on your own, begin by reading the narrative *aloud* to yourself several times, simply to build familiarity. Then, in a calm meditative state, sit with the text open and read it aloud to yourself in short stages (you might like to pencil these in the margins beforehand). During and after reading each stage, build the imagery as strongly as possible. After each stage sit in silence with your eyes closed and see the development of the narrative, its people, places and powers.

Eventually you will be able to work through the induction without the text, or keeping it merely for reference for individual or group work. This unwritten phase is the most important and powerful of all, for it allows for the narrator to improvise and *speak* the narrative from whatever he or she *sees*. At this advanced stage the words of the story follow on from the vision, though for most of us the vision follows on from the words. One note of caution, however, and that is that we should always stay broadly within the aim and pattern of the narrative, and not get carried away by extraneous or silly intrusions. Simplicity and clarity are always the keynotes, working within the tradition.

(A cassette recording of all the visualizations in this book, with original music, is available from Sulis Music, BCM 3721, London WC1N 3XX, England.)

The Basic Underworld Visualization

(If you have already worked with this exercise from *Earth Light* you can proceed to the longer visual narrative on page 35.)

If we reduce the basics of empowered visualization within the Underworld to a very simple working, we have a pattern which may be worked in its own right or into which specific images or intentions may be woven.

1.   A period of silence.

2.   Affirming the Four Directions (see Figure 11 p. 123).

3.   Visualizing a circular closed door or hatchway in the floor before you. If the working is done with a group, they sit in a circle and collectively visualize the closed doorway in the centre.

4.   Open the door, with a clear affirmation of your intent to enter the Underworld and seek the Light within the Earth. If you wish to reach a particular location, zone or specific contact, define this now.

5.   See a steeply descending spiral stair, curving to the right. This stair is cut out of natural rock. Along the wall on the left hand side is a thick rope woven of red, black and white strands, fixed into the rock by stone or bronze fastenings. Descend the stair.

6.   The stair descends into a cave, chamber or hollow within the Earth. Sometimes this is a simple underground temple. Usually you pass out through an archway under which a small lamp hangs, shedding a faint guiding light. In the chamber within, you pause in silent contemplation. At this stage various contacts may be made or visions experienced.

7.   Return through the archway and ascend the stairs.

8.   Climb out through the circular doorway and close it behind you. See the doorway fade into the floor of the room in which you began your visualization.

9.   Discuss if necessary, and make notes.

Notes

If you intend to work regularly with the Underworld tradition, you will find that simple note-taking can be helpful, but it need not be lengthy or obsessive. The most valuable things to note immediately on finishing a visualization, either in private or at an outdoor site, are the following:

1.   Any symbols upon the door or over the archway.

2.   Describe the cave, chamber or underground temple. It is usual to begin with a very simple rock chamber, but this often changes aspect into a related location. These spontaneous changes of location are important and you may return to such a place at will. The initial notes will help you to remember details for future visualizations, and for correlating dream work.

3.   Describe any people, beings or objects that appear within the cave or temple during your meditation. Objects that you are offered as gifts are particularly significant, as these are often keys to further working and may be used in separate meditation upon their power and meaning, or as gifts that you tender at later stages of your work.

4.   Describe the energies or power that you experience while in the Underworld, and how these affect you when you emerge from the working.

Dreams

After empowered visualization at power locations or in private workings, you may have unusual dreams. Any such dreams should be noted down and compared with the effects of your visualizations. Once again, it is not necessary to keep a bulky record or detailed notes, merely to be aware of any dreams that you have involving Underworld images and powers, and to compare these with your waking visualizations and visions.

Visualization should be balanced with outdoor work and movement. The origin of pilgrimages and dream journeys to sacred sites is in the combination of spiritual impulse and physical motion. The next exercise, *The Rising Light Below*, is a simple movement-based technique which forms a balance to the intensive still arts of meditation or visualization. (If you have already worked with this exercise from Earth Light you can proceed to page 35, but remember that it forms an essential part of the overall work programme for this book.)

The Rising Light Below

This is a simple but major technique for arousing energy and passing it through your body: the power that rises from the Underworld, the Light within the Earth, will awaken and transform your own energies far more effectively than concentrating in isolation upon your power centres or *chakras*. If you do this exercise once every day and also work with visualization techniques on a regular basis, you will realign and activate your own energy centres rapidly.

This exercise is the mirror-working to those well-publicized techniques which call down light 'from above'. In both cases the energy seems to begin outside the individual (though this understanding changes as you develop your inner powers), but in this technique the light is inherent within the Underworld, often in a latent mode. Human awareness activates the power and draws it up through the body of the land into the human body. The Rising Light Below exercise is most effective while standing, though it may also be done sitting cross-legged, as squatting and cross-legged postures all enhance our Earth contact. Here are the stages, with some brief notes on their development and effect:

1. *Begin with a period of silence and steady regular breathing.* Your arms are lowered, with the fingertips stretched and pointing towards the ground. If you are sitting they may touch the ground lightly or rest upon your thighs. This initial arm position is important, as you will be raising your arms to different positions through the exercise.

2. *Be aware of the point of contact between your body and the ground.* If this is the floor of a room be aware that the building is in contact with the ground, with the land. For obvious reasons this type of exercise is enhanced by working directly upon the surface of the land, or in a cave, basement or underground chamber. By the holism, paradox, or 'law' of reflections and octaves, it also works very well in high places, such as the tops of hills and in tall buildings. Many Underworld techniques are useful for those of us who live in a city environment, as they pass directly through the imbalanced enervating city energy field, which has little or no effect upon them. If you live in an unhealthy energy-isolated building, do this exercise on the roof or in the basement as well as in your own apartment.

3. *Visualize a source of energy just below the ground or floor where your feet or body make contact.* This is usually felt and seen as a glowing ball of light. The upper surface of this energy sphere touches the soles of your feet (or your legs, thighs and buttocks if you are sitting in a cross-legged position) and from its lower surface a strand of light descends into the heart of the land, into the depths of the planet to an unknown source. This is your reflected energy field in the Underworld, normally latent. You are going to activate it, bring it alive through conscious work. Remember that it is part of you, reflected energy which you do not normally access or use, something of which millions of people are completely unaware, even those who practise meditation and energy techniques.

4. *Increase your awareness of this energy sphere:* feel it touching you, move your imagination into it. You may feel your personal energies descending into it, and a sensation of heat where your body touches the ground.

5. *Gradually draw the energy source into yourself.* This is done by breathing steadily and feeling the energy sphere rise through your feet into your body. Your arm/hand position is slowly raised, drawing the energy with it. There are four zones of the body/energy field: FEET/GENITALS/HEART/THROAT (HEAD) (see Figure 11 p. 123). These are our human reflection of the holism of the Elements and Worlds (see Figures 4 and 7).

6. *FEET: be aware of the Element of Earth,* and the matter or substance of your entire body. The energy sphere rises up through your feet, legs and thighs. This is the first awakening of energy within your physical substance. Your arms are still directed downwards, but slowly raised, drawing the energy as they move.

7. *GENITALS: be aware of the Element of Water,* and the twofold

nature of water in your body. Firstly it is the fundamental element of your cells; on a non-physical level Water is the element of creation, birth, sexual union, love, and represents the second awakening of energy within your physical substance. Your arms are raised gradually to waist height.

8. *HEART: be aware of the Element of Fire.* As the energy sphere rises, it gradually becomes more incandescent. The Four Elements are simultaneously literal and metaphysical. At this heart level the increasing rate of your energy becomes fire. In your body this is bioelectrical energy, the flow of blood and the subtle forces that radiate from your life core. As these subtle forces manifest they appear in an increasingly watery and earthy form. The incandescence of the energy sphere rising from the Underworld through your body is the third awakening of energy within your physical substance. Your arms are raised, palms upward, to shoulder height.

9. *THROAT (Head): be aware of the Element of Air.* The energy has now risen to surround your head and shoulders (see Figure 11 p. 123), and has reached its most rapid and mobile rate. All four zones are now alive, each rising level through the body being holistically within one another. Yet the elevation of energy towards the head causes an increase in rate, and changes of your consciousness. Your arms are raised above the head, palms upwards.

10. *Returning the power.* Simply reverse the sequence by steadily lowering your arms and feeling the power pass down through your body. It returns steadily to your energy sphere within the land, below your feet. As it descends, you lower your arms, and each of the four zones gently reduces in activity.

Meditation Within This Technique

As this is an energy arousal technique, you need not pause and meditate within it at all. Meditation, however, will greatly enhance the effect and will put you into conscious awareness of the energies in and through your body. Pausing for meditation works best after you have developed the raising and lowering technique in its own right. In other words, do not use this exercise and begin to meditate upon each of the four zones in depth before you have completed the full cycle several times.

You may meditate upon each zone as it rises, or as it

descends. As this involves arm movement, remember that you will feel tension in your arms and body. These tensions were used in ancient temple training as sources of power, and the arm positions have a strong effect upon the flow of energy through your body.

AN ESSENTIAL NOTE.   When you raise the energy sphere to the Throat/Head zone, hold it there. This is the most ecstatic zone in terms of meditation and there is often a tendency to lose some of the simple control. Your arm position and tension serve to keep the energy field in the head zone. You should not move into any predefined awareness, imagery or any other means by which the energy sphere rises away above your head and disperses. Remember you are drawing up the subtle force of the Underworld, and of your own being reflected in that realm, and not making an offering or seeking to share or disperse your energy as you might in religious devotion or sexual ecstasy.

You may feel an ecstatic sense of union, have visions of stars, and most of all, a response from the light above which is the consciousness of our Sun as a spiritual being. If you do experience this (and though many people do, not everybody does), do not rush off into it, as you will simply lose your energy. Always aim to pass the power back through your body: anything that is harmonized from the Direction of Above will flow with your intent, and pass through you into the land.

So little conscious work is done today with the land and the Underworld realms that circulating energy in this way is an essential work of sharing, transformation and affirmation of the spirit inherent in matter.

When your energy sphere is returned to the latent position, reflecting just below the ground, you will find that your awareness of the land, the natural world and of many subtle energies and beings is enhanced. Finally, as always, make some brief notes.

The next stage of this energy working is to pass energy in and out of specific locations, objects and other life forms, such as plants and trees.

The Underworld Visualization

A short period of silence is kept before the narrative begins.

First, we build before us the vision of a door set in an aged stone wall. The wall is overgrown with ivy and moss, and the stones are almost hidden by wild growth. Behind a hanging strand of dark green ivy, we see a small low door set in an archway. The keystone of the arch is inscribed with a symbol [*see Figure 10*] which we meditate upon briefly . . .

Now we consider the door itself: it is of dark wood, almost black, hard enduring oak. Upon the door is carved a small image of a bear standing upright, with one paw resting against the trunk of a tree. The tree spreads its branches over the head of the bear, which seems to be turning its head towards us. This is one of the door-ways to the Underworld, and the Bear is the first guardian upon the way. Before entering the door, we must meditate upon the meaning and power of the Bear . . .

As we meditate, the door slowly opens to reveal a low passage-way with stone-lined walls. A small lamp hangs from the corbelled roof, and by the light of this lamp we see a flight of well-made steps sloping gently down. A steady warm glow radiates from the walls of the stone corridor and the roof just touches our heads as we enter. As we begin to descend we see ahead of us another lamp; we realize that these lamps are fixed at regular intervals along the roof and that it is their light that reflects from the surrounding walls.

Behind us we hear the sound of a door closing, and for a moment it seems as if we also hear a large creature moving outside the door, as if something has come to stand guard and protect our backs. We descend the steps and the air seems to be growing warmer. The descent is long and we find a steady rhythm to our downward motion, each step being of equal height and width. This even pace carries us onwards until we feel that we are deep underground.

Suddenly our surroundings change: we pass through a hanging curtain of tiny shells, feathers and bones. The well-jointed stone-work and the evenly spaced steps cease; above our heads the lamps become less frequent, and we see that they have changed into small crude clay bowls, smoke blackened, each emitting a gentle golden light from a single wick. The steps are now rough and have shallow depressions in the middle, as if worn by many feet; there is a gradual spiralling of the passageway to the right, and the shaped stones of the walls are replaced by natural rock. The passageway narrows, and we find a stout rope fastened to either wall by heavy bronze spikes. The end of each spike is shaped into the head of a dragon holding the rope in its jaws. As the steps grow steeper, we use this rope to help our descent: in the dim light we see that it is plaited from three smaller ropes, coloured red, white and black.

The rock walls are tinted an iron-red and seem to be both damp and warm. Ahead we can hear the sound of running water, which grows louder as we spiral round and down. The roof becomes very low and we have to stoop; just as it seems that the passageway is about to close entirely, we squeeze through a narrow gap, and find ourselves in a high-domed circular chamber. At last we can stand freely after the long descent, and we find ourselves upon a smooth, perfectly flat stone floor, cut directly from the natural rock.

All around we hear the sound of flowing water and the air is hot and moist, with traces of steam, but no water can be seen. The chamber is lit by a large silver lamp hanging from the centre of the roof upon a chain. The lamp is shaped as two intertwined serpents each with a wick issuing like a tongue from its mouth, joining together to burn as one single flame.

By the light of this lamp, we see that figures are carved out of the rock, reaching from the floor to the roof of the chamber. There are seven figures around the chamber walls; we pause and consider each one, and meditate briefly upon their appearance and meaning. They are in the shape of seven women, each carrying a different object, each looking strangely human yet non-human. Their feet seem to merge into the chamber floor, the very tops of their heads look down out of the roof; above each head is carved a tiny star from which crystals reflect the light. As the figures are of different heights and are placed irregularly around the chamber, the stars form a group or constellation around the central chain with its dragon lamp.

As we meditate upon the carved figures, we hear a slight sound and then the tapping of a stick upon the stone floor. A figure emerges from behind one of the carvings; he is an aged man, walking with the aid of a silver stick. He has long white hair and a clear pale face; his eyes reveal a long life of experience and compassion.

Without pausing to greet us in any way, he indicates that we must immediately follow him, and crosses to the far side of the chamber where he stands against the wall and watches each of us closely as we approach. When it seems that we can go no further, he strikes his silver stick against the foot of one of the carved figures and a slab of stone tilts upwards behind him to reveal a further passage. As he leads us within, we know that he is the second guardian upon our journey.

The passageway ahead is lit by dim smoking torches set at irregular intervals into the wall; our guide moves very quickly and we dare not pause for a moment. The air is now growing hot and occasionally the entire passageway seems to tremble slightly. Distant deep rumbling sounds are heard and suddenly our guide pauses at a division of the way.

To our right is a wide rounded passage, with the rock fused almost into the appearance of glass; from this passage heat and red light issue and roaring sounds as of a vast creature bellowing in the depths. To our left is a steeply descending passageway in total darkness and the guide indicates that this is our proper route. He stands to one side and with his silver stick points first upwards to a sign carved over the doorway, then downwards into the dark.

We approach the entrance and see that there are many steps glowing very faintly in the shadow, giving just sufficient light for us to feel our way carefully downwards. One by one we enter the passageway, and as we do so the aged man reaches into a plain brown bag hanging at his belt and quietly gives each of us a small object. There is not enough light to see what this mysterious gift might be, so we keep it safe for the future.

Once the opening of the passageway has been passed, our eyes begin to adjust to the dim glowing light from the steps, and when we can see enough to proceed, we begin our next level of descent. Behind us, now far above, we hear a solid thud as the stone door from the circular chamber swings closed. We know that our guide has returned to his watch.

At first the steps spiral around tightly to the right and we turn with almost every step. Occasionally the spiralling stairs still tremble from some deep vibration, and we hear a booming sound that seems almost to contain deep voices chanting or roaring. Down and round the steps turn, round and ever downwards. They become shorter and steeper, merging into one another, until the way ahead turns into a smooth rapidly descending slope. There are small hand-holds cut into the rock walls on either side: we may choose to slide or crawl.

As we move downward, the distant roaring fades away and the air cools gradually, until it is fresh and invigorating. Without warning we come upon a long cyclopean block of roughly hewn stone, making a vast lintel across a low, pitch dark hole. As we crawl through, we find three huge steps, so steep that we have to climb carefully down each one, feeling our way in the dark, for they are deeper than the height of a man or woman. As we climb down the third and last step, we know that these are all that remain of a temple raised up in the most distant unknown past, and that we have reached the very lowermost point of our long descent into the Underworld.

Now we can smell the sea and hear the lapping of tiny waves upon rock. We see faint light from the distant cavern mouth and a long stone landing place cut out of the side wall through which we have climbed. Moored to a stone post is a small black boat without mast or sails.

Behind us we hear a grinding, shuddering sound as the massive rock lintel slowly lowers itself to seal the passageway. There is no other way but forward, and we must climb into the boat if we are to pass into the Underworld sea. We carefully go on board, each taking a seat until the vessel is balanced; then we pause to contemplate the unseen ocean that lies ahead in the light. [*Here music may be played.*]

The vessel moves and we are carried forward towards the cavern mouth, slowly at first but with increasing speed. The water slaps against the prow, then builds into a rushing wave that foams past, flashing with phosphorescent colours in the dimness of the cavern. The arch of light ahead grows closer, larger, brighter, until we break out suddenly into a wide sunlit sea.

The waters are green and blue, with many strange fishes sporting and leaping from their depths; great flocks of birds wheel and cry above us, and in the distance we see a chain of tiny islands. Looking up at the flying birds and the brightly lit sky, we see to our amazement a full panoply of stars. All the constellations shine strongly, each glowing like a jewel with a different colour. This is the sky of the Sun at Midnight, where light and dark, night and day, are perfected in one another . . .

As we watch the stars swirl and move far above us, we realize that the vessel has ground to a halt, her bows resting lightly on a pebbled beach. Before us a steep island rises, set about with many tall standing stones. We climb from the boat, which slides back into the waves and slowly heads out to sea. The island is silent, with only the sound of the waves swirling gently about its beach. There is a faint path that leads between two tall standing stones, and we see a familiar constellation positioned exactly over the gap between the stones; this is the path that we must follow.

As we approach the stones, a figure in a long cloak and deep hood appears from behind the left-hand stone. Her cloak is of deep black lined with red, and her face is stern, partly hidden in the shadow of her hood. She stands before us and holds out a plain wooden bowl, chipped and cracked with age. We know that she is asking each of us for the unseen gifts given by the old man in the distant circular chamber, and we take out these objects for the first time and see them by the light of the midnight Sun and stars. Each one of us has a small disc of coloured stone, and on it is an image representing that which we are most attached to in our lives; this image may be surprising, for it is sometimes not what would be expected.

To pass between the gateway of the upright standing stones, we must give our tokens to She Who Waits. One by one the brightly coloured engraved gemstones fall into the dull wooden bowl, and as the last stone is dropped in, we see a sudden transformation. The dirty, cracked begging bowl seems to flow and twist in the hands of the hooded figure: she opens her arms and it hangs for a moment in the air, suddenly radiating light, set about its rim with jewels, engraved with gold and silver and crystal. The vessel emits a complex musical tone, made of many harmonics weaving together; we see that the patterns are those of the constellations and the jewels on the rim are the Sun, Moon, and planets. For a moment it seems to grow and dissolve simultaneously, then with a last chime, both the bowl and its bearer vanish. We are left to pass freely between the gate, and we find a long meandering path leading to the centre of the island.

The path weaves between many marker stones of different sizes and colours: some are tall menhirs of green granite, others are crude unshapen boulders, while other tiny crystalline rocks have delicate symbols carved upon them. The rambling convoluted way leads between marked stones from different ages and cultures, in a web that we cannot fully understand, sometimes doubling back upon itself yet always leading towards the centre of the island. We follow the path carefully until we reach a single huge upright stone in the very centre of the island. It points directly to a small cluster of stars, and here at last we rest on the heather, grasses and tiny white and yellow flowers that grow in that place. Lying back, looking up at the cluster of stars, we meditate upon this central sacred stone, our position of rest. [*A short period of silence is allowed here.*]

As the stars wheel overhead, they seem to merge slowly into one another until their revolving patterns blur and fuse together into a sequence of silver, blue and grey. This flowing colour surrounds us and gradually solidifies into a circular chamber above our heads, in which seven carved figures lean over, seeming to look curiously down upon us.

We find that we are lying in a circle upon the floor of the rock chamber that we left so long ago. At first we see only the carved figures with their calm strange faces, then we realize that there is someone standing in the centre of the circle, behind our heads just out of immediate sight. We rise to our feet and turn to look upon a youth, who seems at first male, then female. We find it difficult to look fully at this youth, for he or she shimmers and changes face and colour. As the young one smiles we feel a surge of power and take joy in something nameless, yet utterly known to us all. There is the sound of a chiming bell [*here a small gong or bell may be struck*] and the youth reaches up towards the dragon lamp; as he stretches his hands to the lamp, we hear a great roaring and hissing from the tunnels below and the sound of a huge creature stirring. The chamber shakes and seven carved figures seem to move their heads to look towards the youth and the dragon lamp.

For a moment we see both a male and female figure unified within the youth, until the beauty becomes unbearable and we cover our eyes with our hands. Instantly the roaring ceases and we look again to find ourselves in an empty chamber. The youth has vanished, but the dragon lamp has turned from silver to gold and the double flaming wicks have become a single blazing crystal. We pause to meditate upon this source of light from the mineral world.

Now the aged keeper of the chamber emerges from behind one of the stone figures. He firmly taps each of us upon the back with his gold and crystal rod, and we know that it is time to return to the outer world. We turn towards the ascending steps and make our long climb back to the tiny wooden door far above. It opens easily and as we emerge we find that we are in a great garden, which seems to be a long familiar place.

The garden is a curious fusion of cultivation and wild forest: there are countless varieties of trees and flowering plants, and all kinds of fruit and herbs and flowers. Many creatures pass to and fro through this forest garden, many birds fly overhead and perch within the branches: none shows any fear of us. In the far distance, down a long avenue of oak trees lit golden and red by the setting Sun, we see a shambling bear walking beside a tall man. The man wears a many-coloured cloak of leaves and is crowned with a head-dress of spreading antlers; he seems to lean towards the bear for a moment, as if they are talking to one another. We long to follow them but they are already far away, and by nightfall we must return to the human world.

Beneath the nearest trees a circle of carved chairs is set; the carvings show tiny pictures of dragons, tunnels, a dark boat and a wave-filled sea with many stars overhead. These images surround the figure of a dancing youth, or perhaps it is a maiden, with outstretched arms, carved into the centre of each chairback. We examine the chairs carefully and we each find one that is fitting, for they vary in size and shape, and each one has a different symbol somewhere upon it that we know and recognize as our own. The Sun sets and gradually the birds fall quiet, and peace descends upon the great garden forest. [*A pause is made here.*]

We finally open our eyes and return to our point of starting; faintly in the distance we hear the closing of a door, and we return to the outer world. [*Music may be played here if required.*]

Conclusion

The three exercises in this chapter will give you the means of entering and leaving the Underworld, through either the short or long visualization, and the means for arousing and settling your energies, through the *Rising Light Below* exercise. The most helpful exercises are the two basic ones, and regular work with these will make the longer visionary journeys (in Part 2) easier and more effective. Both of the basic exercises have the effect of freeing your energies and your inherent creative or inner vision. Other subtle senses of Underworld contact are also developed but there is no detailed dissection of these in the tradition, such as we might find in intellectual literary occultism. The Underworld experiences aim to liberate and unify our energies and perceptions rather than to rationalize and separate them.

The longer induction narratives also act to liberate and transform, but are designed to lead to specific realms. By this we should understand not only states of consciousness and energy, but realms of being inhabited by others. We can communicate and exchange with these other beings, and the exercises and visions in Part 2 enable this interaction.

In the following chapters, before further practical work, we look in detail at some of the effects of the Underworld Initiation, and the teachings and experiences associated with the Power within the Land.

3. Regeneration, Revision and Reversion

THE UNDERWORLD AND 'KARMA'

Working with the Underworld Initiation is seldom easy, especially as many of the contacts, interactions and events that arise should not be pre-empted by advance discussion or preliminary teaching. Most of all it is a tradition of direct experience.

There are, however, some aspects of the Underworld and types of individual reaction that can be examined in a contemporary context. In this chapter we will consider the experiences of *regeneration* through *revision* and *reversion*. These 3 Rs of the Underworld Initiation will be defined as we proceed.

Because the Underworld is often experienced in terms of what seems to be the past, especially in the early stages of initiation, we may relive old and powerful patterns. In some people this takes the form of memories of what seem to be past lives, which will, after their arousal, work through phases of the present life, until they finally come up to date and coalesce with the apparent present. This process is what I have termed *revision*. Figure 3 shows the cycle at work.

This initial scenario is merely an outline, and to come to a clearer understanding of how revision, reversion and regeneration are linked together, we can describe a classic complete model. Before doing so, it must be emphasized that such an ideal or classic set of experiences will not arise for everyone, and should never be sought after or used as any kind of measure of so-called progress.

The idea of working through and reliving life phases, especially injurious (traumatic) experiences, is well established as a

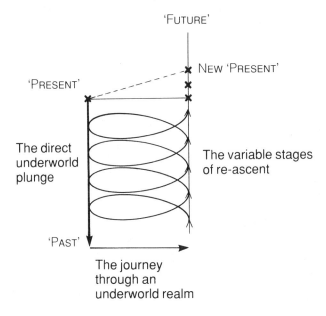

Figure 3 The Underworld Experience

feature of psychotherapy. It has been known for millenia, appearing in many forms prior to modern therapy: two quite different examples familiar to most of us are the Roman Catholic system of confession and absolution, and the Buddhist path of non-attachment through meditation. In the pagan traditions dreams were a major form of therapy, usually in the form of dream induction rather than retrospective discussion.

The Underworld and Earth Light tradition has several differences from any of the above, though all deal with the transformation of consciousness. Perhaps the most significant difference between a psychological approach and the Underworld techniques in terms of a present and immediate life is in the speed and intensity of revision. Upon deeper levels, Underworld experiences open out memories and revisions that are either unknown in modern therapy or are actively denied any validity as they do not fit the materialist psychological model.

Another modern therapy that acknowledges revisions as key experiences is homoeopathy. The appropriate remedy will resonate with a key phase or event and trigger a short experience of 'time travel' in which the individual relives, briefly, a pattern from earlier years which is clearly identified. This transient intense occurrence is the most obvious example of *reversion*, and we will look at this in its Underworld context shortly. Reversion occurs frequently but invisibly or unconsciously in many day-to-day situations, but here we are focusing upon conscious awareness and the connection to deep and powerful patterns of energy.

Reversions can untie knots within us, unravelling energy that has been convoluted into repetitive or self-reiterating patterns. The most difficult aspect of this unravelling for us today is the intentional dissolution of the mask, the aggrandized personality. All spiritual traditions teach that this breakdown must occur before genuine transformation and regeneration will happen. Revisions can lead to understanding of patterns carried over from other lives, usually in terms of the past but not entirely limited to previous personalities.

A classic all-inclusive model of revision, reversion and regeneration through the Underworld begins with the initiatory plunge. Simple methods of entering the Underworld are found in Chapter 2, in *Earth Light*, and in Part 2 of the present volume. Our reactions depend upon the depth to which we enter, usually identified as realms, such as the faery realm, or more isolated locations such as hidden temples and zones occupied by the inner orders or convocations.

We should always remember that this experience is not a psychological one, nor is it confined to our imagination. Though the psyche generates images, either as responses or in empowered and defined visualization, the encounters are as real as, say, running into a rock or falling in love. There is always a physical aspect and an interaction between entities . . . ourselves and others. Due to many factors such as religious manipulation and conditioning, contemporary humans often live in a state of isolated aggression, seeing all other entities as potential enemies. The wisdom traditions associated with the Underworld teach that the human awareness and the planetary awareness are within one another, of one another. In this holism many other beings live and interact: some are acknowledged by modern humanity, many are not. We have excluded ourselves from this reality and withdrawn into a materialist delusion, self-fulfilling and self-destroying. Ironically it is materialist science that has finally realized and defined the planetary threat of aggressive exploitation.

When we enter the Underworld we are not exploring our separated selves or our subconscious, but moving our spirit or true core and source of energy and consciousness into the planetary mind. When we go into the land and the planet, we are entering into a reality that changes us by unravelling or breaking down our delusions of isolation and antagonism. We learn, for example, that dualism is a tool rather than a demanding tyrannical condition. This discovery alone is immeasurably valuable, and it is only one of the transformations possible within the Underworld and Earth Light traditions. Our ancestors depicted the Underworld as a source of riches, both material and spiritual at once. This truth has become lost or rejected by us, but we can recover it. The quest for the Grail is one expression of the story of recovery.

Entering the Underworld involves merging our spiritual reality with that of the planet: the planetary reality resonates with that of the Sun, which in turn is one of the stellar entities. The ancient model of Three Worlds, Moon Sun and Star, represented by the Axis Mundi or Middle Pillar of the Tree of Life, is far more than an outmoded geocentric cosmology (see Figure 4).

When we enter the Underworld our plunge triggers energies, which usually manifest initially as psychic events, though they can and do work right through our bodies. These events open areas that are usually closed to perception and the field of accustomed consciousness. Thus we gain access to those regions defined as *unconscious* by modern psychology but these are both thresholds and matrices for further changes of awareness and the effects of the Underworld Initiation do not come exclusively from either an individual or a collective unconscious. To put this another way, the energies liberated by Earth Light resonate through the so-called unconscious, which can give them either individual or collective pattern and form.

The classic Underworld experience involves a deep plunge into the planetary mind, and there we encounter other orders of life and share ancestral or collective awareness in various ways (see *Earth Light* and *The Underworld Initiation*). On the way back we discover what seem to be memories of past lives, usually of powerful experiences happening to ourselves.

We often relive these seemingly past lives with terrible intensity, and they can bring realizations concerning people and patterns in our present life. This class of realization should be

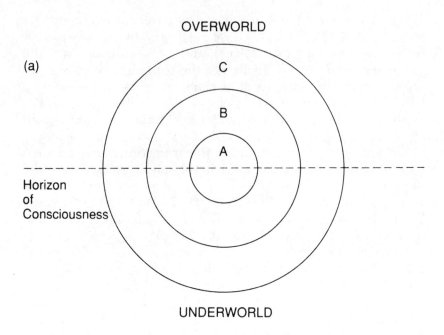

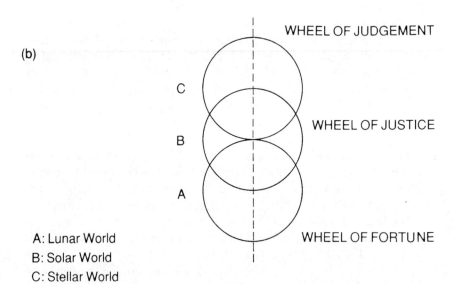

A: Lunar World
B: Solar World
C: Stellar World

Figure 4a The Three Wheels and Three Worlds
Figure 4b A: Lunar World
            B: Solar World
            C: Stellar World

handled delicately, for later (sometimes much later) we realize that these lives are all one life. This new understanding must arise from within, and not be limited to intellectual play or become a clever rationalization, reduction or any other type of comforter. There is no suggestion here that the past lives are fantasies built from elements of the present life, but that the past and present are not separated in the way that we often assume (see Figure 2).

After the deep revision and reversion we return to the seeming present, which does not exist. That threshold present when we entered the Underworld is already in the past, and the present to which we return with our substantially enhanced memories is in the seeming future. This may all seem rather obvious, but in our context of a plastic time pattern that may merge what are usually assumed to be separate past and future, it has to be described. The plasticity of what we describe as time is a function of the planetary mind, in its relationship to the Sun and stars: there is no cosmic clock but a countless flow and interaction of entities and awareness. During the climb back from the Underworld we awaken and relive a range of memories and experiences, eventually working through those of our present life which have built the mask of the personality and which resonate powerfully with our past lives. As we cross back over the threshold of the Underworld Initiation, we regenerate into the future.

Already we are realizing more than one time-scale, which is our true situation with regard to time for we live upon many interacting time-scales at once. What is more, we can choose to modify our awareness of them, and even modify the time-scales themselves. If you enter the Underworld or faery realm by working with the exercises in *Earth Light* or in this book, the threshold of return is, superficially, when you complete the exercise. This is why such attention is always given to ways of going and returning in magical and spiritual disciplines, so that we are certain of our regular everyday functioning and relationship to the consensual world, the shared outer reality.

But having moved from that outer or upper superficial world through meditation and visualization, through the inherent power within the land that enhances our own when we go into the Underworld, we are changed. The return aims to bring us back to operation in the shared world, but we are no longer limited to that world. Upon an inner level we are still aware of the Earth Light and are still, upon another and less fleeting time-scale, moving through the Underworld. It is upon this inner level that we begin our real return, in which the inner and Underworld power arises and eventually transforms the outer and surface world. It first flows through us, then into the world.

So the classic Underworld Initiation cannot occur in a situation where there is total continuity: we all still have habits and situations, life patterns and relative awareness in the shared 'present'. Even if we were able to undertake the classic Under-world experience, of entering and re-emerging through the levels and lives in a trance (as was often done in the ancient and ethnic initiations), this would not obviate the present life. Indeed, I think that, for modern humanity, trance work is not valid, for we are involved in bringing the deeper awareness through into the outwardly focused consciousness, individually and collectively. This has to be done through fusion and empowerment of the faculties and not through dissociation and separation with loss of memory, as happens with trance. Why should memory of the other realms fade? It is our inherent power, so let us bring it alive in our outer life.

Our outer lives, perceived from that tiny proportion of our awareness that generates the collective reality that most humans share in some way or other, become disrupted through Underworld experience. This breakdown is initiated (started) through intent and comes in various ways as a result of any spiritual transformation. The transformations of the Underworld are rapid and intense, through the amplification of the power of the land itself. In effect we may find ourselves diving in and out of the Underworld, apparently spontaneously but actually as a result of continuing resonances from our first willed entry and initiation.

How does this show in daily life? The simplest effect is one of reversion, where we relive some pattern that we recognize from an earlier phase of life: it can be a repeated event or type of event, or a mental and emotional reversion. This is the psychic realm that is focused upon in materialist therapy and psychological theory, though there is increasing evidence that such therapy may not be as beneficial as has been claimed.[4]

With reversion triggered by inner work, we retain our intent and, through the wisdom tradition, can experience the changes without being completely swamped. Sudden reversions are, nevertheless, often distressing and intense, for they bring to the surface memories that are, through Underworld and Earth Light power, indicative of liberation.

Unless the deeper levels are active, simply remembering and rationalizing events is inadequate and this is one of the failings of modern psychology. In therapy such reversion is often brought out through repeated sessions of exploration and analysis, which may or may not have a truly cathartic and regenerative effect. There is frequently that false liberation arising from a psychic structure of rationalizations and based upon dependency or, more subtly, upon the affirmation of having been through therapy. This is rooted in that debilitating mass obsession with affirmation, qualifications, accreditations and authoritative approval. It comes, quite directly, from the patriarchal antagonistic religion of political Christianity . . . are you saved or damned, qualified or unqualified, winner or loser?

None of this pernicious nonsense applies in the Underworld where the Earth Light is inherently our own, if we are able to enter into it by losing our false selves. Sometimes these false selves resonate through many life-times, and sometimes the deep revisions available in the Underworld show us that our contemporary false self is in temporary conflict with our true nature enacted in memories of other lives. The idealized process of revision, reversion and regeneration will apply in as many variants as there are people consciously entering the Underworld.

The process described above will usually come embedded with inner contacts, though often we cannot relate to these until the re-emergence is complete. In the next chapter we return to the theme of contact and communication with the first direct quoted teaching from an Underworld contact.

4. Voices and The Three Conditions

Before our first communication from an inner contact within the Underworld, which is in itself a teaching about spiritual communication, I feel there should be some outline of my own experiences with contacts. These experiences have been many through the years and this brief summary is not a full autobiographical sketch, for it only covers topics and events relevant to the Underworld tradition and the hidden contacts, orders and temples. This introduction to a substantial Underworld teaching will also help to clarify the difference between mediumship, or channelling as it is now called, and mediation, seership and inner listening. These subjects are also explored in Chapter 5.

When I began meditation and magical work in the late 1960s, the idea of contact and communication was less popular and less commercialized and misrepresented than it is today. With certain exceptions it could be found in its most trivial form in spiritualism, where well-established methods of mediumship used large amounts of vital energy to produce reassuring gossip. The exceptions were a very small number of healers and mediums who could and often did deliver something worthwhile out of the general ambience of prattle.

During my youthful visits to spiritualist churches and my personal meetings with various mediums and healers, I gradually realized that the energy drained away by the so-called spirit guides was far greater than whatever they offered in return. Later I learned that these spirits are relatively harmless phantoms or *lemures* that exist in a vampiristic relationship to some humans, if encouraged and allowed to do so. Only rarely do independent spiritual beings with full consciousness speak through or with such mediums and phantom-parasites.

It took me some time to make this distinction, beginning with the obvious conclusion that as the spirit guides offered such drivel, they were either of low intelligence or intentionally misleading the gullible public. I was not bothered about the element of fraud in mediumship, as it seemed clear that many mediums would resort to performances (which someone else would deem fake) and well-established routines. This performance aspect does not preclude other levels within the show providing information from non-material beings. Often the routine is needed to 'warm up', just as a musician might practise scales or an athlete do exercises.

It was during this exploration of spiritualism that I became conscious of some of my own abilities and subtle senses, though these were not trained for several years, and during deep magical work they were turned off. This experience of the psychic senses being stopped is significant . . . it has to happen if we are to move beyond superficial or retrogressive psychism. Later they come back, but in a transformed state.

I found that I could feel the presence of 'invisible entities', and that I was aware of their attempts to drain energy during spiritualist services and 'readings'. I discovered intuitively how to stop them draining my own vitality, and later found that it is possible to cut off a medium's spirit guide and stop its activity. I found that many mediums can be switched from message to message, contact to contact, and realized that the whole thing was lacking in depth and direction. If I could stop a so-called spirit guide, what possible value could they be? It seemed that most of them were limited entities, mimicking human awareness and eventually replaying themselves, like audiotape loops.

In later years I encountered a number of trapped humans, personalities that remained on the threshold between physical death and the necessary psychic dissolution that follows. These were altogether more complex beings than the spirit guides with their absurd claims, repetitive messages and constant leeching of energy. But at the time of which I write, I had not had any such encounters, though I knew that the entities involved in spiritualism were not what they claimed to be. Nor, it appeared to me, were they what they often seemed to think they were (such as eternally discarnate pastiches of human personalities or stereotypical wise men who are ready to deliver pseudo-wisdom at the drop of an astral hat). We shall return to the delusion of the wise masters later, for they frequently appear in other contexts, though generally in the context of mediumship or channelling as it is now called.

Most important of all, I realized that mediumship, both in its operation and effect on others, was essentially degrading to the human spirit. If what the spirit guides had to offer was true then humanity was spiritually doomed to wandering in astral flower gardens, heeding the advice of buffoons in white robes. If it had not been for my undoubted experiences of energy and image transfers in the presence of mediums, I would have found the whole show rather sad and false.

Oh yes, I almost forgot to admit that I saw a few of the so-called spirits too, though not often and only in places where specific beings had been repeatedly visualized and their image forms well nourished. I was not seeking to be a medium but to understand the experience of contact. Interestingly the more coherent spirit guides always told me that I should be a healer as I 'had the power', but this was something that I was not interested in.

I think that the two or three years in which I occasionally went to spiritualist services or had meetings with mediums and healers helped me to clarify my own understanding of my psychic energies (as they were at that time in my life) though not through any acceptance of spiritualism itself.

With regular meditation and magical disciplines, all the psychic stuff stopped. Gradually I became aware of a very interesting process, which was partly explained to me by the man who was, for about four years, my occasional teacher in the Western tradition. The process was this: certain types of meditation and ritual cause surges of energy, and momentary flashes of exaltation or enlightenment. These illuminations are wordless, formless, impossible to reduce to prose. On the way back to normal or habitual awareness, the energy takes various forms within the consciousness.

These forms can be images or visions and can act, with or without images, as interfaces for contact, for communication with other beings. This is different to popular channelling or mediumship, and the contacts are of a very different kind.

Most obvious to me were two facts: these contacts from the magical tradition had something interesting to say, and they never took any vital energy. I learned that this type of contact

was a feature of the Western tradition, and that certain magical orders had specific enduring contacts. (This subject is
described rather romantically by Dion Fortune in her novels,
and to this day the group that she founded works with very
individual and advanced contacts, who may also be met
directly in inner dialogue by anyone working seriously within
the Western tradition.)

I eventually moved from my human teacher to learning from
inner contacts, and most of the material that I have worked
with and subsequently published has been developed from a
combination of these inner sources and my own judgement
and folly. We will come to the Underworld contacts shortly,
and again in Chapter 5.

Many of my first teaching contacts were not of the Underworld, as far as I know, but they were part of an enduring
wisdom tradition spanning millennia. I would like to emphasize that such contacts are regarded as *normal* in the tradition,
though there is a long habit of discretion when talking about
them, for all the obvious reasons. It has never been an exotic or
romantic experience and the tradition teaches us that inner
contact is as normal as outer, once the initial barriers of conditioning have been broken.

In contrast to this quiet approach, in the last decade anyone
with the slightest contact has felt an almost evangelical need to
publicize themselves, and channelling has become a lucrative
craze. Much nonsense is talked about breakthrough and an
upsurge of contact, but there are many people who have worked
with contacts for years without any urge to declare it. Inner or
spiritual contacts are not an end in themselves; they are just
one aspect, although an important one, of tradition worldwide.
They are, in fact, a means rather than an end, though I am not
sure if we can ever divide interaction into a linear process of
means and ends.

In the Underworld the contacts have less emphasis upon
tuition and more upon direct experience. It is the interaction
with the inhabitants of the faery realm, for example, that
causes changes of consciousness and energy. Any teachings
tend to come from ex-humans who have already taken the
way, and are willing to pass on information. Many Underworld contacts are co-walkers or allies with no verbal communication at all, and this situation has its parallel in other
magical or spiritual traditions. Many entities find our type of

communication too slow and ambiguous, and there is a range of symbolic systems that try to cope with this problem.

With practice, however, the difficulty eases and the cumbersome interfaces are done away with as our inherent skills of imagery and consciousness are opened out. A clumsy analogy might be that of learning a new language and then throwing away the dictionary that slows down communication. The best way to learn any language is to start speaking it, even if you only know a few words and phrases. When I started magical work I learned correspondences, tarot alphabets, numbers on the Tree of Life, and so forth, though in retrospect it all seems to have been unnecessary. And I contacted entities who used these symbols to communicate, but this encumbered method soon wore off and we began to talk more directly.

I found that good inner contacts are simple and unpretentious; anything or anyone that appears in a white robe with a tootle of trumpets or suchlike is a delusion or a sham. There are plenty of fraudulent spiritual masters in the meditational realms, perhaps more than there are in our outer world. One of the irritating trials of the sensitive meditator is that of shooing away the quacks who come bustling along when you begin your spiritual quest. In this confusing early situation, a bad or even a corrupt *human* teacher with real abilities often appears briefly in your life as a corrective balancing force.

Most genuine inwardly-contacted spiritual teachers offer firm advice, clear tuition and a stern no-nonsense approach to our own selfish attitudes and lazy ways. The reassuring sweetness-and-light merchants are useless to any student seeking wisdom. After all, when you wish to learn woodwork, a teacher who tells you not to worry, and that the chisel will never cut you and the wood will shape itself if you only wait joyfully is not much use. Spiritual arts and disciplines are very similar to the manual skills and crafts, but upon another spiral or octave of awareness.

UNDERWORLD CONTACTS QUOTED IN THIS BOOK

In the material which follows I have written out as closely as possible, with little or no editing, a teaching sequence from one of my ex-human Underworld contacts called Contact 3 or 'C3' for reference. There are at least two of these quoted in this book and they teach variants of the tradition. Both are found within the state of consciousness defined as the Second Condition (see below), from which clear instructions and teachings may be recovered. The source for the following sequence is what modern esoteric writers call an 'inner plane adept', but in this case an adept of the Underworld Initiation and Earth Light traditions. This teacher only came into contact after my initial and unsettling Underworld experiences which are described in *Earth Light*.

In Chapter 6 I quote from another teacher, 'C2', who gives information founded within the spiritual tradition that bridges between paganism and faery lore and the primal Christian impetus, as found in the old Celtic Church that appeared first in Britain. This contact is concerned with restoring the myths of Lucifer, Adam and Eve, and Christ to their original meaning, and shows how to activate the restored uncorrupted myths within ourselves. This contact also made a large contribution to my essay *The Grail as Bodily Vessel*, first published in 1982 and reproduced in Appendix 3.

When I mentioned above that there are at least two ex-human contacts quoted in various ways in this book I was not being coy or obscure. There are the two described, one pre-Christian and pagan and one Gnostic or Celtic Christian. There is another contact of human origin within the faery realm, whom I have described in other books and who has occasionally spoken to other modern seers, especially Scots.[5] Sometimes these contacts overlap, due to the interaction process described shortly, in which one voice elaborates upon another.

Finally there is another ex-human individual, 'C1', of whom I can say very little, but who is the most powerful contact of this type that I have experienced. The brief instructions on pages 98–9 are from this source, for whom empowered action and direct experience are all and elucidation or expanded teachings are irrelevancies. All of the contacts described are heard inwardly, speaking from different depths. They are all male, though I do not attribute this to my own gender.

There are, however, some strong female contacts in the Underworld and my own encounters with these are typical of the tradition. There are individual priestesses of the Dark Goddess, who seem to be ex-human yet partake so much of Her that they are also non-human, as if their humanity was transformed while they were still in the human world. There are the deeply hidden orders, such as the Sisters at the Back of the North Wind, and a way of contacting these women in the Underworld is given in Chapter 9. They are barely human, in our contemporary sense, but are more powerful than the priestesses of the cavern, pool or temple, for they work in the depths of the planet.

Then there are faery women, of which the ordinary human male is advised traditionally to beware, particularly in sexual encounters. Yet the encounter with the Faery Queen (see *The Underworld Initiation* and *Earth Light*) is essential for any man seeking the Power within the Land.

VOICES AND THE THREE CONDITIONS

In the following extract, the word *conditions* refers to states of consciousness, but also refers to conditions of being, to states of existence. No firm distinction is made between the two in the Underworld tradition, where locations or realms (dimensions) are created by the interaction between the consciousness/energy of the land, zone and planet (power of place) and that of its inhabitants (power of people). By inhabitants, we mean all beings within the land and within its Underworld dimensions, all the living creatures, human, and other orders of life, that *people* a location. Some locations, such as sacred sites and anonymous power places, expand into many realms in the Underworld; other locations will have a less complex inner pattern. Whatever the relative complexity of a place or its people, the three conditions described in the received teaching which follows may be experienced.

Voices (from C3)

There are voices within voices. We partake of a spoken tradition with no books. The first voice, if you are able to hear it, is the simple and powerful source. There are others which elaborate and elucidate, and it is possible to listen to one voice or another, and to ask for elucidation if you wish. The listener and seer may also rework the words, but there are some tales, verses, phrases and powerful words that should not be changed. If you change them, even if you try earnestly to clarify them, they lose power.

All of our teaching and tradition may be received, arising as simple words and visions from the depths, with other voices adding to the stream as it rises. The source teachings are heard by the listener as distinct voices with recognizable tones, and all additions cover these voices or mask their tones, even though they develop their stories.

Such received words come to you from three conditions [see Figures 5 and 5a]. Most voices heard in the silence come from the third condition known as the Voice of Many, and even this condition is closed to people living only on the surface. When the ear is opened first there is a great babble and roar as of a crowd or a battle. In this roar some voices are heard immediately and distinctly, while others are faint and confused. This sea of many voices may be heard briefly as you fall asleep, but is lost when you cross the threshold in either direction. It may also be heard as an intrusive muttering by some when they first enter the silence, but if this muttering is pursued, it slips away.

There are those who ardently seek to pursue the Voice of Many, and desire to have contact with the speakers and mutterers. This is like snatching words from a multitude, or thrusting through a great throng and inviting them to come to you. Those at the edge will jostle to reach you at the centre, while those at the centre and closest to you will hasten to the edge in the press of the crowd pushing inwards.

The third condition is like a sea of echoes from the voices that you have heard since childhood, but it is not limited to your memory alone, for it holds an ocean of memories. As a child learns to shut the ear to all voices and sounds but those that have meaning in life, and to respond only to sounds within certain zones of distance, so must you. The zones of close, intermediate and distant are reversed in importance in the Underworld. There the furthest and deepest voice is the most precious, and the nearest may be ignored.

The second condition holds the voices of teachers. They communicate a steady flow of clear tuition, either as instructions for your work or as tales and verses. They will also issue images and glimpses of places with the words, for those that see. One listener may hear several teachers or only one, but usually a small number, well defined. The experienced seer and listener can distinguish between voices and can attune to them by choice and at will, rather than by chance. This condition is known as the Voice of Few. These are sometimes heard as clear quiet voices that speak close to your ear, though faery beings are also heard in this way.

The first condition is like the voice of the land or, if you are strong, the world. It speaks through deep places and appears to the seer as certain of the older gods and goddesses. The first condition will also utter directly, with prophetic power. When this prophetic power flows through a particular place, it also speaks directly through the prophets and poets of that place, as with Merlin and Taliesin. This is called the Voice of One.

In ancient temples the priestess would remain within the sacred enclosure of earth or water and wait for the voice to utter through her. The oracular priests and prophets, however, were wanderers, often driven wild by the Voice of One. This indicates a truth concerning the Mystery of Man and

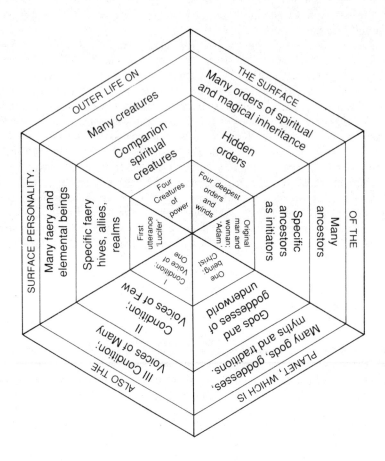

'The Goddess is present through all strands. This Earth-Web mirrors the Star-Web, and is attached to the Sun by a strand from its centre. The Sun-strand is used by beings reaching into the heart of the planet from the Sun and stars.'

Figure 5 The Weaver's Web

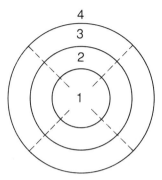

1 = 'Voice of One': core voices and inspiration

2 = 'Voice of Few': specific teachers of tradition

3 = 'Voice of Many'

4 = Yourself, embodying all three

Figure 5a The Three Conditions

Woman and the Sacred Land. This is the truth that was to be turned aside by the story of Adam and Eve.

The direct voice is frequently confused in the mind with the Voice of Many. People who hear for the first time assume that they are hearing a deep spirit or an elevated spirit, when they are only hearing babble. The Voice of One is rare, and talks in potent riddles, in words heard by the body and the soul more than the mind. When it comes to the prophet or sybil the whole body utters it with voice, tears and movement.

This whole utterance should never be confused with possession by spirits: the Voice of One casts all talkative spirits away, and can even destroy them if they are insistent. When the Voice of One is heard the Voice of Many falls silent, and you are set free of it.

Ancestors

Question: How do the three conditions relate to ancestral communication, ancestral memory, ancestral wisdom?

Ancestral voices may be heard in any of the three conditions, but they are often heard foremost within the Voice of Many. The Summoning of the

Ancestors is not just the opening of ears to the third condition and the Voices of Many, for you may hear that without any ancestral summoning, even though there will always be some ancestral voices present. The Summoning causes all voices heard to be ancestral, and others to fade away, washed aside in the ancestral tide.

The Summoning also gives access to the deep supply of ancestral memories which are as if they are your own memories and not through voices alone. Ancestral memory comes through the range of recovered senses, of sight, sound, smell and touch, and is just as you might touch, smell, hear and see and remember the sensations. It also comes through the range of recovered thoughts and feelings, just as if they are your own feelings. It all comes at once as in a sudden flood.

After this flood of recovered experiences, you will hear their voices. You must wait calmly for the flood to ebb, and remain like a rock. This is why in holy places you hold to your ancestral stone and wrap your arms around it.

When you hear ancestors speaking with the Voice of Many they will cry out for revenge against past wrongs. You must resist this demand however just it is. Yet you may and should feel both anger and sorrow at the wrongs revealed to you. Within the urge for revenge find compassion; feel the sorrows of your people, learn from their suffering, transform it within yourself, for you are their future. This sea of memory can become unbearable, a terrible tide through the soul. Here is where ancestors speaking from the second condition will help, for the Voice of Few is wise.

Ancestors in the second condition will reveal how the sorrows and trials have led to slow changes, how the secret currents of life and the land flow through you and your people over many ages, through generations. One generation or more will cry out for revenge, but beyond their own time they cannot extend unless they are awake in the second condition.

Ancestors speaking with the Voice of Few will reveal the true powers of your people and their holy places, which are not always those assumed and taught on the surface. Voices of the wise do not talk of destiny, race or obligation, but only of families of unfathomed extent and their stones and springs.

Those speaking with the Voice of Few will lead you to other ancestral lines hidden within your main line, and enable you to open the way to those memories also. They will also bring you to the threshold where you shall hear ancestors speaking within the Voice of One, or reveal to you ways by which you shall come to it unaided.

When ancestors speak within the first condition, the Voice of One, they are the land. These are the First Ones embodied within the land, and they are, or become, the prime parents of any and all who live within the land for a number of generations. This number is seven for absorbing into the third condition of the land, in which all voices (ancestors speaking with the Voice of Many) are of that land. Before seven generations the Voice of Many will speak from several lands according to your ancestry.

Some come to the First Ones immediately, some only after seven or more generations have passed and the prime parents may perceive them. Thus it is possible by seeking the First Ones as true parents to pass directly from the third to the first condition. This is one of the Mysteries of imprisonment and liberation that you must enter and pass through within the Underworld.

When you move within the second condition you may have access at will to ancestral lines, either of the land of your generations, or of other lands that they once inhabited. Whereas the first condition voices will be of the land or of other lands according to your generations, and you may have little will over it, the second condition voices are always of the land unless you will otherwise.

Some people have several prime parents in the first condition, making a balanced pattern like petals around a flower. Some have less, forming the shapes of triangle, square or pair only, depending upon their land, their people, and their moving about the world. Each prime parental shape has special abilities that emerge upon the surface: the most flexible and powerful shapes for this present age are those of many or of a pair. In previous ages the potency has been in three and fourfold parentage where lands in the same zone have caused their peoples to move and intermingle. Today the prime parents of any one land and the multiple parentage of many hold the keys to the first condition for the entire world.

Prime Parents and Other Worlds

The prime parents of any one land or of many lands lead the way to the Original Man and Woman, but the prime parents of three or four lands intermingled may close this way. The Original Man and Woman are not of this world at all, so deep contact with ancestors in the first condition leads through the Earth to other worlds. This is one of the Mysteries of acceptance that you shall find within the Underworld, but you are not able to follow its path until you have truly accepted your own land and world.

Ancestral Memory and Reincarnation

Memory of previous lives and ancestral memories are not identical. Ancestral memories are communicated through the blood, but other lives need not be of the current bloodline. Other lives hold patterns that surface in the present life, but ancestral memories do not always hold such patterns. While ancestral memories are of the body, other lives are of the starry nature that utters many bodies, often with varying bloodlines.

With practice you will distinguish between the memories of the blood and the memories of the star of lives. [An image is given here, shown as Figure 6.]

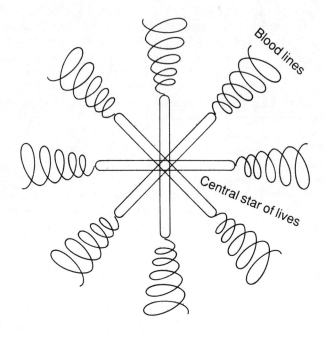

Figure 6 The Star of Lives

In the next chapter we will explore the subject of this type of communication further, before proceeding to other examples.

5. Communication and Contacts

In meeting and experience-gathering workshops, people sometimes ask what inner communication is like: do the voices described in the Underworld teachings sound in our ears? The short answer to this is probably no, not in the sense of a physical sound impinging upon the ear. And not in any pseudo-scientific sense such as the nineteenth-century notion of 'clairaudience', a type of hearing of so-called 'higher vibrations'.

The experience of contact varies from person to person, just as all experiences vary. Perhaps I should say first that in any empowered spiritual experience there is a range of communications or interactions which are sometimes difficult to separate. This often irritates and confuses people who like rigid definitions. If you have studied the rigid definitions and lists of levels of consciousness and planes of existence so widely published, and then proceed to meditate for a few years, you will seldom find anything in your real spiritual perception and changes of awareness that matches them. This is because they are essentially products of the intellect, of word juggling, rather than of experience.

More subtly, our collective awareness has changed since those artificial lists were drawn up by the Victorians, who needed definitions and reduction to order and authority before they could begin any inner experience. So what were the props of our grandparents (and hopefully they knew when to throw them away) become our barriers if we take them literally.

Underworld contact and modes of consciousness mirror the simple but profound cosmology and psychology of the ancient world, where overall patterns such as those of Moon, Sun and stars were defined but the boundaries between them were hazy. In other words, a natural set of iterating and reiterating patterns within a holism. Whatever occurs in Underworld contact, it cannot be too rigidly defined.

The most common experience of contact is in dreams, so we can begin with examples of this type. When I first entered the Underworld it was through a series of dreams, beginning with a vivid and frightening dream which I have described in *Earth Light*. At this time I was living over a powerful sacred site, with an ancient temple to the Goddess underneath my house and the surrounding streets. A major amount of my initiatory experience came through dreams, and later I learned that this was the accepted way of learning and of therapy in the ancient temples.

Powerful dreams were valued highly by our ancestors, and they made sophisticated distinctions between dreams that recycle the waste of our mental and emotional life and empowered dreams which give form to real contact with beings other than ourselves. So how do such dreams relate to the idea of the inner or Underworld contacts speaking to us?

During early stages of Underworld work, powerful dreams are probably the only way in which we can register what is happening. Sometimes they include direct teaching, and such dream teaching is a well-known feature of other traditions also. Later, through the clarifying of the inner vision by various disciplines and transformations, the dream contact becomes conscious. At this stage we begin to identify tuition, the voices, as a separate *form* from inner vision though the *content* may be closely related. In dreams, form and content are fluid and interchangeable. So a vision of the faery realm in a dream may include a voice telling us things as we move through the place, but when we awake we tend to forget. In conscious contact we hear the voice while awake and often see associated visions, but the two are not blurred together and forgotten.

To clarify this further, I will try to describe my own method of working when I write out the material from inner contacts, which is not unusual or unique, but taught and experienced within the Underworld and associated faery traditions. What happens is something of this sort: I enter into a chosen subject or visionary scene, but not too deeply as this will cause the outer faculties of writing and reading to be suspended. Various ways of entering have been described elsewhere[6] so I will not repeat them here. Sometimes I begin by writing or describing in my own words, but rapidly hear a voice speaking on the subject, and I write out what I hear. I do not hear it physically, but inwardly. Sometimes there are voices overlaying one another, with some expanding on the first voice, but always with a choice of which level or voice to focus on. Amusingly this embedding of different levels has appeared in our information technology in recent years, where we can chase a subject through various levels or choose to view it superficially. The inner contact, however, is alive and not a replay of a data bank.

When inner contact is established it is also possible to ask questions, though answers are not always forthcoming. Most of the communications quoted in this book were embedded within visionary scenes. This is how the guided visualizations are made, expanding from chosen scenarios within the tradition, but with new material from contacts and specific inner locations.

In the material from contact 1, who is a powerful seer and Underworld adept, everything is embedded within strong visions, images that are unforgettable, and a sense of personal involvement as if directly experiencing whatever is being taught. The language is terse and evocative, and the voice startlingly clear and yet quiet, with no undertones or posturing vocal inflections.

Contact 2, by comparison, has a more discursive educational and philosophical approach. There is less vivid imagery, though images are used sporadically. Sometimes C1 will break through the rambling discourse of C2, and add a pithy comment or a bright visionary clue to whatever is being described. In my own imagination, and with no proof whatsoever, I feel that C1 is similar to the true Merlin (not the modern stereotype);[7] while C2 is similar to a monk from some Celtic order of very early druidic Christianity. Please note that I do not claim or even think that these contacts *are* such people, only that this is how I tend to identify them. One has to be very careful indeed with such identifications, as they can ruin the clarity of the communication.

What does *not* occur is the following: I am not 'taken over' nor am I compelled in any way. No comments, suggestions or guidance have ever been given concerning my personal life, and if I ask for such I am told to stop complaining and do whatever is necessary. These contacts behave in a very different way from so-called spirit guides or channelled 'Masters' who seem obsessed with interfering in ordinary human situations. They do not push or pull me in any way, and only occasionally do they call me and contact me by surprise. When this happens it is usually possible to store the contact with a key image or word for recovery in later meditation.

I have no idea what the beings that I have called contacts 1 and 2 do when they are not talking to me, and they have never given me their life stories. They come when I tune my mind to them, but I do not command or call them. These are not the only contacts that I work with, but are the most relevant to this discussion and this book.

Both contacts use rather archaic language, but there are none of the literary tricks such as prithees, thees, thous, and no quaint medievalisms or words inserted from languages that I do not know (or even for those that I do know, such as French, Latin or Greek). The words are colourful and sometimes ambiguous, but not forcedly poetic or unnatural. One interesting feature is that when I try to modernize and clarify some phrases, they are often restated in a different way, or replaced altogether. As a rule I have learned not to impose my own editing, though the temptation is strong. There is some leeway in the words of C2 for change through rationalization, but C1 insists that his words are written out exactly as communicated.

So I hear these voices and see their associated images, but do not think of them as products of my imagination. Traditions of such contacts are known worldwide, though Western culture has tended either to neglect or trivialize them. Over the last twenty years I have learned much from inner contacts, both in the Underworld and in other realms or dimensions: they are an essential part of all spiritual traditions.

TALKING AMONG THEMSELVES

We should also ask if the received or mediated teachings are the kind of communication that Underworld sources use among themselves. Almost certainly not, as the communication is filtered through our own conditioned parameters, even when we interfere with it as little as possible.

With practice, the seer and listener discovers that the teachings are expansions or flowerings of concentrated consciousness. Once more we can find a materialized analogy in computers, where data can be stored in a compressed state that expands or explodes (a good technical term) into its restored full version. This analogy only works to a certain extent, for the data on a disk has first to be written in full, then compressed, then expanded back to its original state. In consciousness the reverse is true, for the original state is the concentrated one.

Beyond the most cogent words and visions in both communication and meditation is a deeper core or heart of consciousness. This is described as the First Condition (page 57), the mind of the planet, Ancestral Union, the Awakened Sleeper, and is the state of being sought through the Underworld Initiation. In some ways it is similar to the much advertised 'higher consciousness' of theosophy and New Age enthusiasm, but the Underworld embraces and includes, rather than rejects or denies. The body, of the land, the world, yourself, is the sacred realm, and no flight to higher planes and cosmic union can avoid this truth for long. The Underworld traditions begin by embracing the Earth and end by discovering that its consciousness is universal.

Within the deepest Underworld, communication is direct and almost formless. To us it emerges as rapid flashes or bursts of highly concentrated awareness, which flower and proliferate as words, images, movement. These impulses become more complex but less powerful as they externalize. This is the reverse of our accustomed relationship between consciousness and experience, in which many events and media of communication are distilled into our total experience or wisdom. In Celtic myth the legend is that of the Cauldron, where all knowledge is reduced to a single potent drop over a period of time. This same Cauldron brings regeneration and rebirth, for it is the Cauldron of the Underworld Goddess, and the original Grail (see page 134).

The distillation of much into little is reversed in the Underworld, where simple and highly concentrated awareness and energy are indivisible. This primal condition of unity moves and surfaces in many patterns, through living beings, including ourselves. The simplest powers are the strongest and this is why on entering the Underworld we lose much, and make offerings to the Goddess. What we lose is our surface complexity and what we find is our inner reality. This is the condition in which the various orders of life within the Underworld communicate.

TALKING BACK

So can we talk back to them? If you work with any of the exercises in this book or *Earth Light*, you are already talking, which is to say, interchanging energies. This subject is often confusing, especially when we come from a culture with severe sexual convolutions and imbalances. The quality and quantity of talking back will vary from person to person, and it also changes during our life phases. You can only talk honestly (to anyone) when you have nothing to hide, nothing to be ashamed of, and no selfish ulterior motive. This idea of truth and honesty is at the foundation of our spiritual communication, so in different phases of our lives, depending upon our self-knowledge, we are or are not able to talk.

Many people who read books on magic and spiritual arts and disciplines think that adepts spend long periods of time in trance communicating with other worlds. As far as I know this is not true, and it has never been true other than in the specialist work in ancient temples. This type of temple work is not well suited for us today, as it requires a collective consciousness that we have moved away from in our increasing tendency towards individual awareness.

I do not talk back to the Underworld contacts and allies in the sense of daily conversation, nor do I enter trance states that obviate my regular awareness. There are exchanges that occur, however, in altered states of energy and consciousness: they are not easy to describe as they must be experienced rather than discussed. I have published various methods that you can work through to gain such experiences for yourself, and some of these methods were taught by inner contacts.

After some practice, what eventually happens is this: a rich and varied set of inner experiences becomes active in a continuum, alive and ever-present. When I began to meditate as a teenager, I did so for hours each day. Even now I can hear my teeth grinding, echoing down the years of effort. Although I can now joke about it, never let anyone tell you that meditation is easy, relaxing or even pleasant. There are techniques that induce relaxed and calm states (temporarily) but these are not true meditation, as they cross no boundaries of consciousness and bring no permanent changes. Meditation is very hard work, as any nun or monk in any genuine spiritual tradition will tell you.

Today I do not frequently meditate formally in the sense of sitting down and withdrawing and changing the focus of my attention. But I find that the equivalent of that meditation, and much more, flows in and out of my daily life. This is nothing more than any skill in which years of training bring about subtle changes that lead to effortlessness. In music, for example, the skilled player lets his or her body do the playing, and seldom thinks of the individual notes, fingers, lips, keys or strings. A skilled woodworker moves the chisel beautifully and economically, and has forgotten the time of aching muscles, ruined wood and frustration. And there is always more, for effortless skill is only the beginning.

So rather than being locked in trance or withdrawn into contemplation, I find that things simply happen. Some of my most useful work as a mediator and writer has arisen in railway station waiting rooms, on trains, and while walking in busy streets. The most powerful states of consciousness and energy, the most potent magical events, can be enabled very simply, with no hours of concentration, no rooms full of trappings, no scripts. All of these accessories are helpful to some of the people some of the time, but that's as far as it goes. Working with groups over the last ten years or more, I have found that simple is powerful. And this is how we exchange with the Underworld, how we talk back.

CONTACTS AND CATALYSTS

Esoteric orders, religions, cults and ethnic magic of all sorts, worldwide, rely heavily on their contacts. One of the oldest practices was to have continuity of spiritual contact: a classic example of this is the spirit of the Tibetan state Oracle, a tradition far older than the Buddhism that is now merged with its chthonic predecessor. Even in exile today, the spirit contact speaks through the person of the Oracle, who is what we would loosely call a medium. In Western magical orders, since at least the nineteenth century, certain known contacts are maintained, often identified as adepts of earlier centuries. In folk practices the faery contacts often stay within certain families, and in pagan religion and magic the world over, inherent family powers and contact with spirits, gods and goddesses are handed down through specific lines. This last aspect of contact is closely connected to ancestral awareness and is widespread among primal and shamanistic peoples.

Much of the Underworld tradition, in its original form from the ancient world and described in folklore, is about ancestry, bloodlines and inherent and inherited abilities. While this still applies to a certain extent today, we live in a world where the old isolated cultures are breaking up and merging with one another, and the communal sharing patterns of magical and spiritual realization are vanishing. Furthermore, it just is not enough to rely on your inherited talents, or those of another, in spiritual development. The idea of a family or clan magic is still viable in some ways, particularly in an inner or metaphysical way, but is gradually being replaced by something else.

For want of a special term, I have called this something *catalysis*, as it applies to people whose *presence* enables transformation in others. In science, a catalyst is usually an inert substance that causes others to react, so the analogy is not exact. What happens is that anyone who has undergone the Underworld Initiation can, by being present, enable and enhance the experience for others. In old-fashioned magical orders this enabling through presence was well known, though a closely guarded secret. It was, and is, a remnant of the old lore on genetic and sexual magic. But through active Underworld work, the catalyst becomes conscious rather than unconscious, acting with intent rather than automatically. In Underworld terms, something very revolutionary has happened, for the closed orders, families and clans of our ancestors are opening ranks.

If the catalyst individual is a skilled mediator, all members of a group entering the Underworld with that person become members of a family or clan, usually that of the mediator. Only two or three generations ago this would have been unheard of. What it means is that as more individuals and groups enter the Underworld and make contact with the inhabitants, the shared and exchanged awareness and energy grows exponentially rather than serially.

In my own travelling work with irregular groups in Europe

and the USA, I can guarantee to put an individual or group into contact with inner teachers, faery co-walkers, spiritual creatures and ancestors. What I cannot guarantee is what might happen as a result of such contact, nor would I presume to try, as it will vary from person to person. I can also guarantee to take a group to any Underworld location that I have already visited, and to bring them all back out again. But what happens when they are there is variable, and out of guarantee. This is as it should be, otherwise there is no spiritual freedom, and the Underworld tradition is, above all, one of choice and freedom.

This catalysing ability, conscious or not, and the guiding ability are the same ability that enables someone to *mediate* and to *hear* and *see*. They are not separate talents, but when they are unconscious or inherent they seem to be limited to one expression, such as catalysing or seeing at random. The Underworld Initiation brings these talents back together and activates them. This is through the techniques that cause the Arousal of the Blood, and the awakening of the Inner Fire, by passing into the land, which empowers us. Please note that this is *not* done through meditating on our energy centres or *chakras*, but through entering the Underworld and interacting with its inhabitants (see Appendix I).

Ancestral abilities are usually aroused first, those of a blood line within you. After this come other individual abilities which you have. Once the spectrum of inherent abilities is awakened through the Arousal of the Blood and then the Inner Fire, other potential abilities are opened out. Some of these are opened for the first time, revealing possibilities and realities of consciousness and energy that are not in the ancestral repertoire. These are new human abilities, not dormant or inherent. The effect of the power within the land, of the Earth Light, is to accelerate consciousness and energy but only through interaction and exchange, not as a gift to be plundered. If you work regularly with the material in this book and in *Earth Light* you will experience this interaction for yourself.

In the next chapter, we will explore the theory of the Triune Alliance, a bond between human, faery and spiritual animals. This is followed by an extract from Underworld contact C2, and a discussion of the mystical traditions of Lucifer, Adam and Eve, and Jesus in the Underworld.

6. Regeneration of The World

THE TRIUNE ALLIANCE

To reach the deeper levels of the Underworld and make the contacts that are possible there, we work with companions. These are found in the primal Northern and Western traditions in two classes: spiritual animals and faery co-walkers. Gods and goddesses are not worked with as companions, though there are other magical and spiritual unions in which they take part. There is much confusion current over types of companion, partly as a result of ignorance or prejudice and partly through the widespread revival and commercializing of so-called shamanism.

Most of what passes as modern shamanism would be regarded as ridiculous and trivial by a true shaman within a living shamanistic culture, rather like a costume party with a theme of 'let's pretend' atavism. Most, but not all. Clearly we need to re-enliven the primal arts of magic, which are all about relationship between human and other beings. If we make fools of ourselves along the way it does not matter, providing a few succeed.

While it is clear that much of the Underworld and Earth Light traditions are or were found in true shamanism, folk magic and faery lore and survivals of paganism, this is not the whole picture. The great religions of the ancient world and their high technology of magic also partake of the Underworld stream of tradition, as does original Christianity in its early fusion with the pagan sacrificial cults. Many of the esoteric aspects of the perennial wisdom teachings can only be brought alive through the Underworld.

So in this book, and through the techniques and examples it contains, we work with the lore of the Underworld as it exists in three interconnected sources:

1.   Celtic and European collective tradition;
2.   Classical, Celtic and Norse paganism and associated formal religions and Mysteries;
3.   Oral or subtle teachings and practices handed down to initiates.

The first set of sources includes faery lore, tales and ballads, and many reports and collections over several centuries. The second is found in written sources which have been heavily censored by political Christianity, but still preserve much. The third set includes two important branches which have occasionally found their way into literature: esoteric Christianity and genuine workable magical arts. It is in this third area, which includes received teachings, that we find the lore of the Triune Alliance most clearly explained.

There are hints and obscure references in historical and collective sources, such as faery marriages and companion animals in folklore, myth and legend, and a range of interesting complaints and ineffective thunderings from orthodox religion. As late as the seventeenth century, the Reverend Robert Kirk[5] wrote that his Gaelic parishioners were wearing themselves out with faery lovers rather than attending church. Kirk, however, inherited the blood of faery alliance from his mother and was a seventh son, and therefore, according to tradition, a seer. Often he comments on the teachings and practices of the seers and faery healers with full knowledge, but disapproving of those aspects which offended official religion. In the nineteenth and early twentieth centuries the Order of the Golden Dawn experimented with faery marriages to balance and enhance energies, and this human/non-human union has long been one of the 'secrets' of formal magic.

More than enough has been published in recent years concerning spiritual creatures or 'totem beasts', which are found throughout paganism and in an attenuated form accompanying saints in various of the older Christian sects such as Catholicism, and the still older Orthodox and Celtic Churches. The Merlin tradition, which is embedded within the Underworld and sacred land traditions of Britain and Europe, uses a range of spiritual creatures extending from the stars through the planet and into the Underworld.[7]

Very little is found, however, of the Triune Alliance. This is not a marriage, and is not a situation in which the human seeks to dominate animal and faery beings. This idea of control and domination is found in various magical traditions, and in literary occultism plays an unhealthy major role. While the Underworld experiences involve many trials, challenges and tests, the tradition does not teach that humanity is superior and must subjugate all other orders of life.

A more subtle form of this arrogant assumption of the human right to dominate is found in esoteric Christian magical orders, where it is assumed that humans are superior to other life forms, be they physical or metaphysical, and if these are 'lower' forms that they must be 'redeemed'. This means that instead of going into the Underworld to meet the Goddess and our beloved brother and sister beings, we must have a hidden agenda of redemption based upon our innate superiority. This, ironically, is the Luciferic sin of pride.

The Earth Light redeems us all, whatever type of being we are, for the Redeemer, who has many forms, is one of the Sleepers within the body of the planet. Yet the Redeemer is also awake among the stars as a universal spiritual being. This paradoxical teaching is discussed on page 75.

However we approach the metaphysics, the Triune Alliance is an equal partnership between human, creature and faery. This forms a balanced team for Underworld work, with each member benefiting from the others. Apart from the practical aspects, there is a subtle transformative effect which is regarded within the tradition as truly redemptive for all participants. This transformation is equated to the reappearance of the Redeemer or Christ as a woman, one of the oldest teachings of Celtic Christianity and preserved in oral tradition for centuries. An inner or received teaching on this is quoted on page 77.

In seeking and finding partners, as described in *Earth Light*, the human initiate enters the Underworld by various means taught within the tradition. There the spiritual creatures meet with the human candidate for partnership, and one or more chooses to approach. Let us be very clear on this matter; they choose us, we do not choose them.[8] The same happens in the faery realm, where on entering a faery hall we find a great host of beings. There are, however, more variables in the faery realm and we may choose not to work with the first or second beings that come to us. After the third we run out of choices, though we may return again when we feel ready.

So the creatures, usually natural forms of land, sea or air, choose us. If we do not like the creature and refuse to work with it this reveals something about ourselves. Most people find that they are chosen by at least one creature. The faery allies are often reluctant to work with humans but usually several will volunteer, as the alliance is a well-established art among them, though partly lost to us. Out of the first three we may choose one primary ally and co-walker. This choice opens the way for other allies. People who insist on choosing potential allies from those who do not come forward are, of course, bad-mannered and arrogant, and misunderstand what is happening. The procedure is given form as a guided visualization in *Earth Light*.

It is customary to work first with creatures, as they inhabit our surface world, then to work with faery beings, then to begin work with the Triune Alliance. This gradual approach, however, may be pre-empted in practice today, though only if such pre-empting occurs naturally within the Underworld. In group work people find that if they enter a faery hall then both faery allies and creatures will come to them. If they work to find spiritual creatures only, this experience does not involve faery allies. So in practice we can go direct to the faery realm and may, if we are fortunate, find both partners there. If this does not happen, the creatures must be found separately.

Let us now proceed to an Underworld communication on this subject, and its relationship to the legend of Lucifer and the regeneration or redemption of the world.

The Perfection of Lucifer (from C2)

One of the operations [of the Underworld tradition] has become known as the Perfection of Lucifer. It is found in the re-uniting of that which has become separate. Here is a key to it.

Three orders of being live within the world, within and not upon, for nothing that lives is of the surface only. They are the human races, the faery races, and the races of creatures within the land, sea and air. Angelic and other spiritual beings that may be known and unknown are not within the world as humans, faeries and creatures, though they may have exchanges with the three orders and be in worlds adjoining.

All three orders are of one another, yet many do not know it and cause suffering to themselves and others through their ignorance. At the original moment of the Bright One [Lucifer] embodied in the Earth these three, once united, were separated out to walk different ways through time, place and power. They seem to have appeared in the world at times vastly removed from one another as if in three separate appearances, but this is due to the mystery of that original embodiment and its triple power.

The faery races, of which there are many in each land, were of the original perfect world unmanifest and retained its starry light when they entered into the Earth. The races of creatures which appeared next in land, sea and air were of the increasingly manifest and less perfect world, yet innocent. Human races, which appeared last, were of the potentially balanced world, found through knowledge, but because the triple power of separation is reflected in a small way in each of them, they are prone to forget. This balanced world of humanity was to be at the threshold and able to cross back and forward at will. Such knowledge is still available, though it is more of an art than a science.

Through unity of the three orders of being, human, faery and animal, the Sleeper in the Land is awakened. This is the way of perfection that is so hidden as a truth that few know of it. The awakening of the Bright One, Lucifer, is not of the land alone, but of the whole world. It is the light of the world shining back to the Sun which is its sister, and each knowing that they are of the stars and united in being.

Three Utterances of Light from the Mother Dark. The first gave substance to the Bright One, who was both male and female. This giving of substance is what is now called the Fall of Lucifer, and when the star fell the faery races also fell into the body of the Earth. To the old ones there was no hint of pride or sin in this fall, for these follies are only human and the stars do not sin. At this Utterance the faery races had bodies of changeable light, and all other forms were mirrored in these.

The Second Utterance made substance of the human races, and this what is now called the creation and fall of Adam and Eve and the expulsion from Paradise. And all such imputations of division through Woman and temptation are wrong, for as the old stories tell us, Woman is the guardian of the way to our true home and not the cause of any fall through sin.

Between the First and Second Utterances, which are the separation of the faery and human races from their stellar union, the Five Zones of power in the body of the Earth lived and moved and made the lands and seas. Out of this movement emerged all the living creatures, and those with faces moved outwards and those without faces moved inwards living upon and within the others. And all beings live as movements out of and into the substance of the Earth and partake of one another.

So the creatures are constantly moving between the faery realms and the realms of mortals, the lands above and below. They aspire towards the knowledge and companionship of man and woman, and yet return to the first and primal world of innocence. And this spiritual movement of the creatures is mirrored in their seasonal passage from place to place. They may still go where mortals are unable to reach, and so the seers and walkers go with them and come back again.

The Third Utterance

The Third Utterance is of the spirit of regeneration, which has many names but is known to you as the Redeemer and as Christ. The power of this Utterance passed not into the land but into the entire world, seeking to pass through the Second Utterance and further in to merge with the First.

When the human, faery and creature races recognize one another and come together again, the Redeemer will have completed gestation within the body of the planet. There is a Fourth Utterance, which for the world is yet to come, and this is the fourth of the great winds of the stars. This Utterance transforms the world into a being of perfect manifest knowledge and open mind, to have no memory but being perfect in present knowledge of all that was past or future. This is the Mystery of the rebirth of Christ as Woman, during the last age of the world.

How shall you come to this wonder, sleeping within the earth yet awake among the stars? When you knock upon the door of the realms within the land, you meet first the prophets and ancestors who have passed within, such as Merlin and the rest. And when you are able to pass through the realms, you will find the Sleepers of each land and of each of the Five Zones. Every location will have its way to the Sleepers, but you must seek ever further in and in.

At the heart of the realms, the heart of the world, is the perfect light of regeneration. This is the united power of the First and Third Utterances, and this too sleeps but for brief awakenings. This Sleeper at the Heart of the World awaits the acknowledgement of the Second Utterance, which is to say the union of all three orders of being within the world. Now you may come to this union and make acknowledgement through intent, through the way of passing within the land and through the realms.

But the union also comes of itself, for the light will emerge and the Sleeper awaken when the period of nurture in the womb of the Earth is complete.

Do not assume, therefore, that you are barred from the light, for if you enter into the power within the land, you will come to the power of the Earth itself. When you enter the power of the Earth, you will come to the light and to knowledge and memory. Whatever is of the world is echoed within you – the Three Utterances are there, and when you unite with the co-walkers of the other orders, faery and creature, the Fourth Utterance will arise from within the Earth and within yourself, speaking at once for both.

Sacrifice

What do you sacrifice to Her but your presumed fall? When She destroys you She consumes your fall from grace, She withdraws this aspect of yourself into Her Body which is grace itself, for the Earth is a mirror that changes whatever is reflected within it. She will cause you to be reborn in a new form, just as the redeeming power of Christ will be reborn in a new form. And if you enter into the power of the land and of the Earth itself, you will find that the rebirth has already come, and only your own separation and forgetfulness keep you from it and from knowledge of it.

The Three Strains

Do not assume that we are talking only of three strains, qualities or types within yourself. Admittedly all three, the human, faery and creature strains, are echoed in you, and how could this not be so, for the Three Utterances are in you. So you mirror the ages of the world.

We are not discussing a merging or assimilation of three appetites, three behaviours, or three classes of mind and emotion, though you may draw many such threads together, and rightly. We mean this: three distinct orders of being, human, faery and creatures, that may unite to re-unite. These are the three strains of our way, the three orders that partake of it. There are others also, who join with us, but for you the three strains must come first.

When the three emerged as distinct entities in a new world, which is a new time and space, the faery race had nothing of humanity in it. The creatures that afterwards generated out of the lands and seas had something of the faery powers, which are of the perfect world, and a little of humanity, such as the possibility of love and partnership. Humanity, coming out of the stars but becoming of the Earth, has all three strains within but has excluded itself from knowledge of the other two.

This exclusion may seem to you to be through the pursuit of knowledge of matter, as if the one type of knowledge bars the other, but it is the effect of the power of isolation and materialization. These are the great mirroring powers that we use to bring change speedily through intent, rather than to be changed slowly and unwittingly. Place a mirror to a mirror and see for yourself. Do you see what animal you have within that you have forgotten, and what animals without are your own partners? What faery blood and tribe shows in your face and form when you look in the glass, and which of the faery hives will appoint co-walkers to you?

Within man and woman the balance of the Four Elements may be found in potential, though it is seldom realized. One way that was long hidden from the oppressors was the marriage of human and faery races, which brings a sexual union and, for the human, weaves the soul and ties it to the faery race for many ages. Beyond that is the Triune Alliance, which is not a marriage, for there is no sexual union, but an intentional triple bond between human, faery and creature. This is an equal and balanced partnership, leading to a revelation.

While the human races have all Four Elements and one or more of these weak, the faery beings have either triple or single Elements, while the creatures have double. Thus the Triune Alliance may have seven or nine patterns of reiteration: it may pass through all worlds, and none may bar its way.

From this communication, we can move on to a further discussion of the tradition, before beginning practical work.

THE UNDERWORLD TRADITION, LUCIFER AND CHRIST

In various chapters in this book there are references to the myth of Lucifer, which has become absorbed into the more obscure areas of Christian dogma and today is frequently misapplied, as if identical to the idea of the Devil. The old Christian mystics and theologians liked the story of Lucifer: as propaganda it taught that if you did not do what you were told then God threw you out; 'pride goeth before a fall'. On a more subtle level it described a great spiritual being who became embodied within the Earth: this had, surely, they thought, to be a *punishment*, a negative key to the undoubted and embarrassing fact that the ancients had drawn spiritual enlightenment from below rather than above. The ancients were deluded, according to Christian interpretation, by a proud archangel posing as the divine inherent in the mundane.

The story of Lucifer is often invoked in folklore as the cause of faery beings, saying that when Lucifer fell, they were drawn with him. Overall it is a myth about the prehuman consciousness of our world, at a time when organic life had not appeared. In Christian and related Middle Eastern beliefs the fall is regarded as punishment and the initial cause of evil through separation and division. So an element of blame and fear is attached to the spirit inherent in matter.

The subsequent development of the Devil is powerful propaganda based upon three main elements: the desert tribesman's *shaitan* or adversary, the intense campaign against the widely revered horned gods of the pagan world, and the myth of Lucifer.

The older spiritual traditions, from before Christianity, also teach that evil is due to separation, isolation and the resulting antagonism. But they do not attribute evil to the spiritual power inherent within matter, which later became known as Lucifer. Evil is rooted in isolation, selfishness and loneliness. All rage and malice and wanton destruction derive from isolation and loneliness. There are higher octaves of evil, which consist of intentional spiritual isolation even when in full knowledge of the holism of universal being. This is often described as the evil of cold intent rather than that of hot rage.

The Underworld is not a realm of isolation but of reunion and regeneration: we return to it either at physical death when our bodies are recycled, or willingly during our lives through inspiration, vision, dedication and the initiatory arts. It is the shortened way both to rebirth and to the stars.

The inherent Underworld power, demonstrated to us superficially by the law of octaves, is that universal consciousness is inherent in universal matter. Now we tend to say inherent in the sense of dormant, but the statement should be that universal consciousness and universal matter are co-existent. The well-known story of Schroedinger's cat, a theoretical but potentially possible experiment in quantum events, is perhaps the most modern example of such understanding.

So perennial wisdom and modern physics both advise that events and consciousness are interchangeable, and that the nature of matter, far from being rigid and immutable, is plastic and malleable in direct relationship to observation, which is to say, to consciousness. If we imagine our world before organic life appears, when it is a world of conscious matter or materializing consciousness; this is the condition of Lucifer within the Earth. This is the first octave of becoming, which is called the First Utterance in the inner teachings of the Underworld (see page 76).

Evil has been described as misplaced or imbalanced energy, with the degree of evil depending upon the perceptions of the observer. In other words evil and good are not absolute but relative interactions out of the universal becoming. Evil is defined by the observer as it relates to the observer's understanding of good. This is why we can confuse evil with Lucifer, for Lucifer is the power of becoming that can seem to rest dormant for millennia but then bring about sudden radical world changes.

Combine our self-preserving fear of deep changes with a

huge and well-designed programme of religious-political propaganda and conditioning over a thousand years or more, and
we arrive at the situation where humanity seeks to control the
Earth, even if it means destroying it. To resolve this problem of
our conditioned antagonism to the Earth, to the spiritual power
in matter, we must *consciously* work to improve our relationship
with the land, its occupants and the planet. This is what the
Underworld Initiation sets in motion.

The old pagan-Christian mysticism taught that humanity was
created to rebalance the fall of Lucifer and those spirits and angels
that fell with him. The purpose was to awaken the dormant
universal consciousness of the Earth through a *mediating* being,
that interfaced between 'above' or solar and stellar beings, and
'below' or Lucifer. If Lucifer is universal consciousness as
matter, humanity is universal consciousness as flesh, as a
collective organic being with high levels of potential separation and individuality. Still universal, still becoming, still living
conscious substance, but a different pattern, a harmonic overtone. This is the Second Utterance referred to on page 76.

However, humans became absorbed in the consensual world
that was becoming, and forgot their divine origin. This is pro-
pagandized as the fall of Adam and the dogma of sin, linked to
the suppression of woman and of worship of the Goddess.
What this really tells us is that the process of becoming tends
towards complexity of pattern, yet seeks always to know itself
through the images within the pattern. This is the Web of the
Weaver Goddess, if we use the imagery of the Underworld.

If we look at the iterative patterns of so-called chaos mathe-
matics, such as the popular Mandelbröt set available as com-
puter graphics, this weaving and self-mirroring is amply
demonstrated. It was stated and perceived in meditation as the
interaction of the Four Elements in the philosophy of the
ancient world, and as the energies of the Seven Directions in
geomantic magic and in metaphysics. Legends of the Weaver
Goddess often involve the spider as her spiritual creature, the
thirteenth sign of the Zodiac.

In the apocryphal legends of Jesus (*Gospel of Thomas*), we are
told that a spider wove her web to hide the infant Saviour from
the soldiers of King Herod, who were seeking to destroy him.
This Saviour or Redeemer appeared to bring humanity into an
increased awareness of the divine, so redeeming not only
Adam and Eve but through them, Lucifer. This is called

the Third Utterance in the Underworld tradition, universal consciousness manifesting directly through the vehicle of humanity, and resonating afresh through the entire planet.

The myth of Jesus is not original but a variant of the profound Goddess-based magic of the sacrificial kingship, involving sacred conception, miraculous (by which we might understand immaculately synchronous) birth, and dedicated death. However pagan the Underworld tradition is, it acknowledges and teaches that Christ was a spiritual being who spoke to the entire planet. Many variants of this teaching are found, from dogmatic Christianity to Gnostic heresy.

The Underworld tradition teaches that while the sacred kings and chthonic heroes of our ancestors were of the various power locations and lands, Jesus was of the planet. In one branch of the Western Mystery tradition we find an interesting teaching: the birth of the world Redeemer was a response, an answer to the many questing spirits of the sacrificial kingship. We entered the Earth and simultaneously sent our souls into the universal Being in search of truth for our people. And in time the universal Being replied, and entered humanity and through us passed into the Earth also.

So Jesus also descended into the Underworld after his sacrificial death, and from the Underworld was regenerated to rise again. The difference is not one of the event, for death and resurrection myths abound worldwide and were fundamental to the pagan world. It is one of identity and degree, of the nature of the being that we call Christ.

Finally we have the theme of the return of the Redeemer, albeit transformed. This is the Fourth Utterance, in which all others are consciously awakened and harmoniously united. In esoteric tradition we find that this return or reiteration is linked to the Goddess rather than the God, and that the Redeemer is to appear as a woman. This may be linked to the curious tradition that man is redeemed through woman, found in some of the Grail legends (see Appendix 3). There is a poetic symmetry here that bears fruit in meditation: Lucifer is androgynous then male (depending upon the tradition), humanity is polarized as male and female. Jesus is male but transcends polarity, reaching to a divine androgyny. The new consciousness becoming aware of itself out of universal matter in our world will be female, but will balance the rhythm of polarities and bring androgyny out of the Earth.

Within the Underworld, realm of potentials and becoming, all of these events or Utterances are simultaneous. They seem separate to us, across great stretches of time, but they are one event, varied according to its self-generated observers. When we enter the Underworld we begin to unify the Utterances.

CONCLUSION

We have come now to the end of Part 1, which has dealt mainly with the essential traditions of the Underworld and has described the effect of their inner reality upon us. Many aspects of these traditions and the truths that they embody have yet to be explored. We are not just regenerating old mystical and magical arts but seeking to restore and develop a living tradition that will change our world and ourselves. Furthermore the changes are not arbitrary acts of human self-interest, but grow out of the interaction between many living beings through the realms described within the tradition.

Modern people are in a paradoxical situation: we have lost the continuity of the old wisdom traditions and need to recover the means of contact, learning and experience that such traditions contain. Yet we can never revert to the collective world that produced such traditions and we must find a way of regenerating them for whatever may be our potential future.

In Part 2 we move into the more advanced exercises and visionary narratives which put us into contact with the hidden orders and temples . . . bearing in mind that these terms are poetic rather than hierarchical or political. The contact will eventually build new techniques through an exchange of awareness between humans and others, but we begin with material firmly based in the collective traditions. But most important of all, the contacts and allies *work with us* rather than just teach or talk at us. We work together to awaken the Sleepers and regenerate the world.

Part 2

Visualizations and Exercises

Part 2 is a collection of practical work with related information. The visions and exercises are powerful and should be experienced in the order suggested in the work programme for this book (page 122). Ideally these exercises should be done after the series in *Earth Light*, but the work programme is arranged to stand alone, with two of the basic techniques from *Earth Light* reproduced in Chapter 1 of this book. The contents of Part 2 should be approached gradually, in the order in which they appear, and within the overall programme. Please do not experiment with the visions out of context, as the same cautions apply to them as we might apply to any skilled work or powerful tool.

7. The Mystery of The Sleepers

In the heretical Grail legends and associated tales and ballads in European tradition, we find the theme of the Sleeper. This is often a wounded knight, king or warrior, though sometimes prophets such as Merlin are also found sleeping. The legend of the Fisher King, within which the wounding of King Arthur is absorbed, is the best known variant from medieval literature. In the *Corpus Christi Carol* or *Down in Yon Forest*, we have the same theme and type of imagery in a ballad from oral folk tradition, where the Grail, or rather the word 'Grail', does not appear and the hallows or power vessels support the wounded figure from each of the cardinal directions. We will work with this ballad shortly.

The tales and songs from collective oral tradition represent the primal images and foundation upon which the medieval literature was based. Oral tradition is of great value when we seek to activate the transformative power of a magical theme; often it indicates powerful images and symbols that were not influenced by literature, as the inheritors of the tradition had no access to texts. The Grail legends may be traced to Celtic pagan sources in terms of literary history, but all versions are underpinned by enduring oral tradition, enduring well into the twentieth century in some examples.

It seems likely, though unproven in a historical sense, that the Grail texts represented an intentional preservation of lore that was outside the accepted range of orthodox Christianity. Another possibility is that those who assembled and formalized the legends sought to Christianize beliefs that were widely held and active in medieval Europe. The two theories are not contradictory.

The Sleeper or Wounded One awaiting regeneration, originally a pagan theme associated with the sacrificial kings and heroes, was broadly linked to the sacrificed Christ. In either case, and with their fusion, the Sleeper and the altar–bed are fragments of an Underworld Mystery. What is most interesting for us today is that whereas the Grail legends declare the central figure to be male and Christlike, in folk tradition we have both male and female Sleepers. We will return to the male sacrifice shortly, when we examine the imagery of the *Corpus Christi Carol*, originally from English oral tradition, but let us first look at one of the most popular of all fairy tales, *Snow White*, beginning with a summary of the story.

SNOW WHITE

A beautiful girl has no mother or father but is brought up by a stepmother who is a witch. Her stepmother seeks to cause Snow White's death, and orders a woodsman to take the girl into the forest, kill her, and cut out her heart as proof. The woodsman (hunter or gamewarden) cannot bring himself to kill Snow White, so leaves her in the deepest forest and kills a stag instead, taking its heart back to the witch queen. Meanwhile Snow White takes refuge with seven dwarves who mine precious metals and gems and are skilled in smithcraft. The Queen uses her magic mirror, which always reveals the truth, and discovers that Snow White still lives. She takes the shape of a crone and lures Snow White into taking a bite from a poisoned apple, whereupon the girl falls into a deathlike deep sleep. When the seven dwarves return from the mines, they craft a wondrous bed of crystal for Snow White and keep constant watch over her body, along with the forest creatures.

In most resolutions of the tale, the witch queen is killed and Snow White is brought back to life by the love of a prince, for only through true love can the spell of the poisoned apple be broken.

The story contains many of the major keys to the Underworld tradition and corresponds with a number of other legends. Let us look briefly at some of the key images from a magical and initiatory viewpoint.

1.   *The Dark Queen:* is found throughout folklore as the negative or taking power. Sometimes she is rationalized as a witch or jealous stepmother, sometimes she is the powerful Faery Queen (see *Earth Light*).
2.   *The Maiden:* is the innocent and pure soul at the heart of the tale.
3.   *The Woodward or Huntsman:* guards the forest and protects the Maiden. He sacrifices a deer or stag as a substitute and takes its heart to the Queen. In some variants the stag volunteers to die for Snow White, for the creatures of the forest love her.
4.   *The Seven Dwarves:* are Underworld or faery companions to the Maiden. As with other allies in faery tales, each has a special skill. They combine their skills to make the crystal bed, to which we shall return shortly.

There are many variants of the tale and this is only a brief summary. Even so, Snow White is the *female* Sleeper of the native tradition of Europe, allied to the creatures and to powerful faery and Underworld contacts. She is associated with the Guardian, who takes the form of man and stag combined, and he protects her through sacrifice. The Dark Goddess with her Mirror of Truth is the power of life, death and transformation.

The Sleeping Maiden is awakened through the power of love, and only a pure heart can pass the Guardian, the Creatures and the Seven Companions. Her wondrous bed of crystal and precious metals reveals the realm in which she sleeps, the heart of transformable matter. To reach her, the lover must leave the human world, represented by kingdom and court, and pass through the great forest that bridges between the animal and faery realms, one of the powerful threshold dimensions of the Underworld. Tests must be undertaken, and in the mysterious heart of the forest the lover finds the crystal bed, manifested from the realms below by the Seven Companions.

A detailed visualization, *The Sleeping Maiden*, using this imagery follows on page 99 and an extract from a direct and powerful Underworld teaching on the theme appears on page 105. The Sleeping Maiden, unlike the Grail or Wounded King legends, is utterly pagan.

THE CORPUS CHRISTI CAROL

(Refrain, sung after each verse)
Lullay, Lullay, Lullay, Lullay,
The Falcon hath taken my make [mate] *away*

The heron flew east and the heron flew west,
She flew over a fair forest.

She flew up and she flew down,
She flew over an orchard brown.

In that orchard stands a hall
Covered all over in purple and pall.

In that hall there stands a bed,
Covered all over with purple and red.

On that bed there lies a knight,
His wounds do bleed with main and might.

From his wounds there runs a flood,
The one half water the other half blood.

At the bed's foot there lies a hound,
Licking the blood as it daily runs down.

At the bedside there sits a maid,
Sowing a seam with a silver thread.

At the other bedside there flowers a thorn
That never so blossomed since Adam was born.

At the bed's head there stands a stone,
Corpus Christi written thereon.

The visualization of *The Hall in the Forest* on page 106 is based upon the pagan-Christian image of the Sleeper, associated with the Grail legends and other esoteric Christian themes with roots far into the Underworld. Many parts of the vision are closely related to that of the Sleeping Maiden, such as the spiritual creatures (hawk or falcon and heron that fly through the fair forest) and the deeper enclosure at its heart. In the *Corpus Christi Carol*, however, we find a dying orchard, in which a great hall has been built around the Sleeper.

The apple, either as fruit, tree or orchard, is the gift of the Goddess, bringing either life or death, as in the ballad of Thomas Rhymer.[2] The withered orchard can be restored when the Sleeper awakens, when his wounds are healed. This seems apt for our present environmental crisis.

The Sleeper here is wounded, and streams of water and blood flow from his wound. In expansions of the vision, we find that these are the rivers of blood and water that flow through the Underworld, which have to be crossed in the journey of Thomas Rhymer and other examples of the Underworld journey.

The wounded man is surrounded by key images, and in the version quoted above we allocate these to the Sacred Directions defined by the orientation of the Bed. While a standing or sitting human defines the Seven Directions as in Figure 7a, a human lying down as in Figure 7b causes the Directions to interchange. This may seem simplistic, but it holds the key to one of the initiatory Mysteries of Sacred Space. It can be broadly summarized in words, but really has to be experienced to be understood. Briefly it involves the changes of consciousness and energy that occur when we are deeply aligned to the Seven Directions, which are our natural directions when standing on the surface of the land, and attune to planetary and solar and stellar forces.

This is not deeply esoteric or obscure, and is found in the many directional energy fields known to materialist science. In spiritual and magical arts, the Directions extend into realms of consciousness and if we attune to them, remarkable changes can occur. There are two ingoing or withdrawing states associated with lying down: sleep and death. The two outgoing or creating states are sex and birth. When we are upon our backs (and any variation of horizontal rather than any variation of upright), the natural directions are interchanged. This simple and obvious fact is used in energy changing work in many spiritual traditions, where body positions alter awareness and energy flow. When we find it in the Mystery of the Bed, we have a fusion of spiritual, geomantic and sexual Mysteries.

Surrounding the Sleeper (Figure 8) are the following:

Bed foot: a hound, licking the flowing blood. Spiritual animal of the Wild Hunt, of death and the Underworld. In overlays of courtly love symbolism, represents faithfulness.
Left side: Maiden or woman sewing a silver thread. The Goddess of Life and Death with the thread of Becoming. Overlaid as mourning lover.

(a)

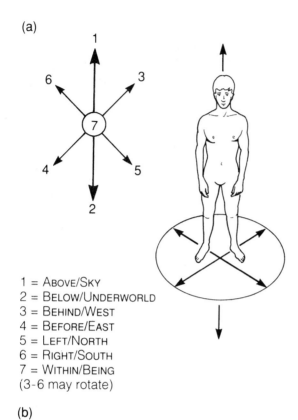

1 = ABOVE/SKY
2 = BELOW/UNDERWORLD
3 = BEHIND/WEST
4 = BEFORE/EAST
5 = LEFT/NORTH
6 = RIGHT/SOUTH
7 = WITHIN/BEING
(3-6 may rotate)

(b)

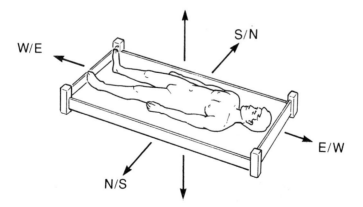

Figure 7 The Sleeper and the Seven Directions

Figure 8 The Sleeper

Right side: Blossoming thorn tree. The thorn marks the threshold of the Underworld and is associated with the Goddess and with faery contacts. Complex and important overlays are associated with sacrifice and regeneration. The thorn blossoming for the first time since the birth of Adam tells us that the Sleeper is of the sacred blood line, or is understood as Christ (see also Appendix 3). But see Chapter 5 for the Underworld teaching on the successive Redeemers and the relationship between human, animal and faery beings.

Bed head: A stone inscribed 'Corpus Christi'. The inscription refers to the stone itself, which marks the head position of the Sleeper. The body of Christ is united, consubstantial with densest matter. The sacred stone is at the Head position showing the interchange of Above and Below.

In some variants of the ballad we find different orientations and there is no 'authoritative' version. One of the open secrets of magical and spiritual arts is that once we have worked with the alignment of Directions, Elements, Powers, they can and do move. With sufficient time and practice working with Sacred Space and the energies, major images and contacts will appear in different directions (see *Earth Light*) with differing effects.

AWAKENING THE SLEEPERS

The female Sleeper is awakened through the power of love, but we are given no hint as to the awakening of the male Sleeper. Both are associated with the powers of life, death, sexuality and regeneration, not simply of humanity but of the land, the planet and all the interwoven orders of being and their worlds.

The awakening has to come first within ourselves. The Mystery of regeneration (or redemption, though the word is loaded with unfortunate propaganda) is understood in many ways, all beginning with our own intent to redeem and regenerate ourselves. The Underworld tradition indicates a way towards this deep transformation, through the Power within the Land, passing within according to potent techniques handed down within the tradition itself.

8. Awakening the Sleepers

We can now move on to two major visions, of the male and female Sleepers as described by tradition, with appropriate induction narratives. Before these, we work with a technique known as *Diving through the Moon Pool*, which is described here in three variant forms. Each has its advantages and we begin with a basic version using a Tarot trump or other suitable picture image. Next comes an advanced version, in which a physical location or sacred site is used. The third variant is the original teaching from which the others have been adapted. This original teaching is a powerful example of techniques taught through direct Underworld contact, and should not be attempted literally without real experience, skill and understanding of its implications.

The original Moon Pool teaching (variant 3) makes no distinction between outer and inner worlds, physical and spiritual realms. The basic exercise for contemporary use (variant 1) relies on a protected or undisturbed period of visualization, working entirely in the inner worlds. The advanced exercise for contemporary use (variant 2) fuses inner and outer worlds, involving both vision and physical location, but still distinguishes between them. Although the third variant is the most powerful and is the original, we work towards it through the other two, which give us a gradual development and many safeguards against over-extending our awareness and energies.

Diving Through the Moon Pool

Variant 1

1. Begin with the trump of The Moon from the *Merlin Tarot*[9] or any other suitable Tarot deck where this trump includes a pool. Become familiar with the image until you can see it clearly and steadily with your eyes closed. If you are experienced in working with trumps, you should be aware that each trump has 'secret' paths and gates, which are not the ones used in our well-established meditative, visualizing or pathworking techniques. The *Merlin Tarot* is recommended because the Underworld paths and gates are readily accessible through its trumps, but most decks will work.

2. Build the image strongly and with your imaginative power, dive into the pool. This should be an intense experience, invoking all the sensations. Work at this until you can dive in and climb back out easily. Do not plunge through the pool to the other side until you have worked with the experience several times. An enhanced method is to practise regularly in the nights leading to a full moon, then take step 3.

3. Plunge through the pool, diving deeply. Some people find it easier to dive in and swim to the other side. You emerge for the first time in another place. If the vision is uncertain at this stage, build it with your imaginative powers as follows:

> You emerge at a crossroads. One road leads out of the Pool behind you, and three more are in front of you. The road to the right leads to a wide plain lit by flashes of Earth Light like wild fire darting out of the ground (see Figure 9). The road to the left leads up to a steep mountain from which streams of water flow. The road before you leads to a wild dark forest.

Work repeatedly with this vision until it becomes clear: dive in and out of the pool until the three roads are instantly visible when you arrive. The vision will gradually develop in detail with each visit. When you are ready, follow the road into the forest, using the detailed visualization narrative of *The Sleeping Maiden* which begins on page 99. Do not take the other roads until you have experienced the forest.

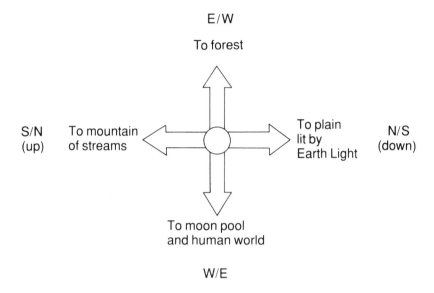

Figure 9 The Crossroads and Mingled Directions

Variant 2

This is an advanced version of the method, in which you choose any one of the three roads.

Do not attempt this method until you are experienced in Underworld visualizing and visions. Before you work with this, you should have a good contact established with companion creatures and faery allies. The method seems simple but requires skill, stamina and the Triune Alliance (see page 72).

1. Become familiar with the visualization of diving into the Moon Pool, through working with the trump of The Moon. You should have already experienced a range of Underworld and faery contacts, and used the Moon dive for admission to the forest and witnessing the Sleeping Maiden (see page 99).
2. Use the Lunar cycle of preparation described in *Earth Light*, and on the full Moon find a reflective surface to work with. If you are working indoors you can use a mirror or bowl of water to reflect the Moon. If possible, find an actual pool or lake where you will not be disturbed.

3.   Do not use any written or recorded source, but focus your awareness upon the reflection of the Moon in the mirror or water. Use your power of vision to dive into it and emerge at the crossroads. Three roads are before you:

- The road to the right leads to a wide plain lit by flashes of Earth Light like wild fire darting out of the ground.
- The road to the left leads up to a steep mountain from which streams of water flow.
- The road before you leads to the forest, but you are now able to make other meetings there or seek other contacts.

You can travel any or all of the three roads, though you would usually travel only one a month.

Variant 3 – The Original Moon Pool Ceremony
(from inner teaching contact C1)

Fast for three days before the full Moon. Remain chaste and clarify your sight ensuring that no shadows are in it. On the night of the full Moon go to the pool alone. Take with you a treasured possession to give to Her. (If the Moon is covered by clouds stay for a time in silence and return home. Begin again with the next full Moon.)

When you come to the pool look first at the Moon above. Circle the pool three times and acknowledge the power of the Four Winds. Sit with your gift and recall its story, then throw it far out into the pool. Watch the water until the ripples cease and you can see the mirrored Moon. When you see clearly, remove your clothing and dive naked into the pool.

Dive deep and swim swiftly to the other side. When you emerge you will be at the Crossroads. Choose a road and when you have chosen, a Guide will appear. Challenge the Guide if there is no speech or sign and only standing still. If the Guide challenges you, instantly answer with your first impulse and truth. If the Guide is hostile, call upon your co-walkers to appear, and the Guide will change form or be replaced by another. Do not threaten the Guide or attempt any force. Your co-walkers will talk with the Guide for you if you cannot.

If no Guide appears, choose a road and walk it alone. Do not summon co-walkers, but reserve their aid for the return if necessary. Walk or run rapidly and fix the way in your mind, avoiding all distraction. Do not leave the road until it ends. (Some hear calls of love or screams for help from the surrounding lands and see their loved ones or their enemies out of the corner of one eye. This is a false encounter from failing to clarify the vision and clouding the mind with low dreams during the three-day fast. These false sounds and sights are from within yourself and take form briefly out of the power in the land. Do not follow them and they will cease.)

In the place that you come to, you will find your gift terribly changed. At first you may not know it, but by signs you will come to it. You must mould it into a new form by whatever means you can, summoning your skills. When that form is complete One will come to you and destroy it with an Element. At this moment both destroyer and destroyed will vanish. At this moment you may meet Her. Be ready.

Return by whatever way to the pool, by the reverse road or another that is shown. When you reach the pool dive in and swim to the other side. When you emerge do not look at the sky. Wait watching the water until the ripples have ceased and you see the mirrored Moon. Now look up at the sky, dress and return home.

The Sleeping Maiden

Begin this vision by diving into the Moon Pool, using Variant 1 described above. At the Crossroads you will find a small mirror, a comb and a pair of shears or scissors. Take all three with you along the path to the forest.

From the path out of the Moon Pool we come to the edge of the great forest, a mass of dark green trees and shadows. As we approach we hear the rise and fall of sound from leaves stirred by the low wind, a surging and whispering. The light is dim and falls into darkness by the trees. We feel uncertain about entering this great forest, for it is alive, and even from a distance we sense its strength and watchfulness.

Now we are within a few paces of the outermost trees; three more steps and we will enter the forest. We take the first step and there is a sudden thunder of wings as a flock of dark birds erupts out of the branches and flies off deep into the forest. We take the second step and hear the sounds of many creatures rising up and moving away from us through the undergrowth; we cannot see them but they move lightly and swiftly away, so we know that they are deer. Now we are crossing the tree line and with the third step, the entire forest falls silent. Out of the silence we hear the faintest of sounds, and a stag steps from behind a huge oak tree to stand before us.

In the dim light we see tall spreading antlers and the stag seems to tower over us. We feel his breath touch our faces, and smell his strange vital scent. This is the Guardian of the Forest and he will only let you pass if he is certain that your motive is to bring no harm to the place and its inhabitants. In his calm presence we feel a sudden flow of memories, a rapid sequence of all the injustice that we have done to the land and to the living creatures. We feel ashamed and angry, and swear upon the great oak tree that we will resolve such injustice, beginning within ourselves. One by one we set our hands and foreheads against the tree, and swear. Deep within the trunk we feel a slow rhythm, moving to a vast flow of time that we had almost forgotten, within which our own lives seem minute and fleeting.

When we have sworn, we see the Moon appear through the branches high above us, and clouds passing slowly across her face. In the shifting moonlight the stag turns and moves away into the darkness of the trees, towards the heart of the forest. We follow as quickly as we can, stumbling in the dark, roots tripping our feet, branches snatching at our clothes and hair. Sometimes the Moon reveals the narrow path winding through the trees, then her light is masked and we feel the way, sensing the presence of the stag ahead of us.

With this sense of what is before us, we find that subtle night vision comes alive in us. We see the great trees and the forest floor in faint hues of grey and dark blue, of black and silver. Now our other senses come alive with nightpower, and we smell the earth, the resins of the trees, the damp air full of life. We also smell a faint sharp perfume, like green sap and rich wild blossoms, and our hair begins to rise as if electrified. We keep moving after the stag, and the scent blows to and fro in the soft wind. Now we hear, emerging from the other forest sounds and the noise of our own movement, a faint brushing through the trees all about us and we know that large creatures are keeping pace with us.

We hear breath blowing out, the stamp of hooves and a faint muffled ringing of harness bells, and suddenly we see that we are surrounded by riders on grey horses. The riders have long flowing hair and carry white spears. They look at us and laugh, and the sound of their laughter fills us at once with both longing and terror. One by one the faery riders approach, urging their horses towards us and crying out in soft high voices. We see that they are male and female, and strangely beautiful: as they approach their scent changes and we smell a deep and powerful perfume filled with sexual warmth and hinting at ecstasy. We feel pulled to go with them, yet long to run away into the tree shadows and escape.

Each rider chooses one of us and cries out in two voices, speaking right into our minds. One voice cries: 'Come away with me, beloved, away beyond the forest to the Halls of the Ever Young, come away and live in joy and light beyond the Sun and Moon, where the clear rivers run and there is no pain, where the wide grassy plains stretch forever and are filled with flowers'. And another voice, yet the same voice, cries: 'Foolish ugly mortal, run

from this place, for here is terror and despising, here are all your lusts and stupidities laid open. Run, corruptor and destroyer of the blessed world, run from the lances of the faery host . . .'.

As we hear these voices we still ourselves and enter into Silence, not closing down but opening to the deep Peace that is beyond and before all movement. [*Silent meditation here.*]

Now we emerge from the Silence to see the riders hurl their spears at us, straight at our faces, and we dive flat onto the forest floor. There is the sound of horses galloping and a surge of wild laughter, then silence and stillness. A shower of ice crystals falls upon the back of our heads and necks, and we feel a strong urge to laugh at ourselves. When we look up, the faery riders have vanished. It is time to resume our quest.

As we move forward the forest thickens, until we push and squeeze through thick young growth between massive aged trees. Here the generative power of the trees has run riot, creating a surge of growth and decay that we have never seen in our own world. The Moon rises above us and we see ahead a wall of thorn bushes laced with flowering wild roses. They bar our way, and as we realize this, we realize also that the stag has gone. Beyond this high thorn hedge is a mystery . . . we feel its presence, yet can find no way in. Far away under the moonlight, an owl calls.

We try to peer through the thicket and see within faint flashes of light where something glitters and reflects the Moon. Suddenly we remember the small mirror that we found at the Crossroads. Holding it up to catch the flashes from behind the hedge, we see a momentary image of a figure lying on a bed in the centre of a moonlit clearing. In the mirror we can see a way through the thorns, though when we turn and look directly the thicket seems impenetrable. To enter the clearing we must move backwards through the thorns, and when we do so, they give way slightly to let us pass. Yet if we try to turn, we are held fast.

The further we move backwards into the clearing glimpsed in the mirror, the more the thorns wrap around us. We cannot turn or move forward into the forest that we have left, and must follow the inevitable reflected way, through moonlight, shadows and brief flahes in the mirror. [*Short pause here.*] We fall backwards onto grass, and for a few moments lie still, feeling foolish, relieved and exhilarated. Now we stand and look around the clearing.

The Moon shines out, suddenly bright as clouds pass away, and in the centre of the clearing there is a brilliant flash of white light. We see there a bed made of crystal with silver lines inlaid in a web pattern. Upon the bed is a young woman, still as death. Her beauty is painful to see, and the sight of her still form in the moonlight brings out memories. From deep within rise terrible memories of

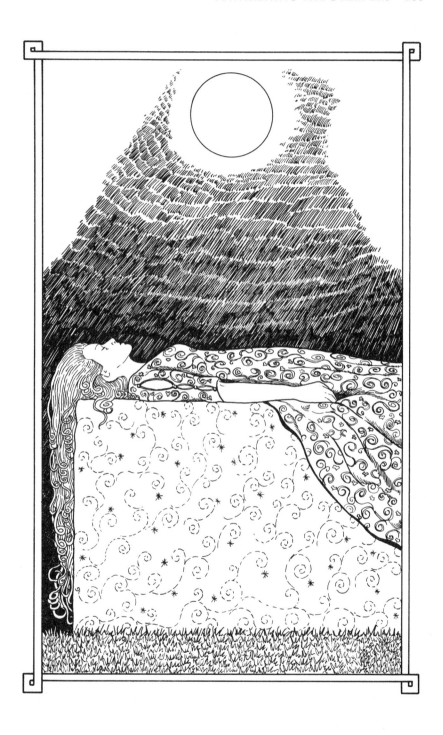

every unworthy aspect of our lives, of our inmost selves, and we find that we cannot approach her.

We look upon the calm wonder and beauty of her face, then see that she wears a long white robe with green tendrils woven into it. The sinuous green pattern mirrors the silver web within the crystal slab that makes her bed, and while the green bears tiny leaves and buds, the silver bears stars. Looking upon the figure lying on the crystal bed we are filled with lifetimes of longing, of sorrow, of regret.

As these feelings flow through us, we know that we must find a way, within ourselves, to approach the Sleeper. In silence we search within our hearts for an answer: what will enable each of us to approach her? [Short pause here.] The answer is simple: remember your first love, the first man or woman that you know truly loved you, other than your parents or family. Hold to the truth of that love, untouched by regrets or sorrows. That moment of recognizing love is a moment of power, of life, living in you still, found with another person but beyond all personality. The recognition of selfless love within another.

One by one we feel the deep sorrow pass from us, and approach the crystal bed. As we approach, dark figures emerge from the thorns at the far side of the clearing, and we look for the first time upon the Seven Companions who watch over the Sleeper. They are beings of great power, each with a special skill, filled with the wisdom and purpose of the Underworld. One Companion comes to each of us, and asks for either the mirror, comb or shears. As we hand these over, they change through a variety of shapes before becoming still in the hands of the Companion.

Though you picked up mirror, comb and shears at the Crossroads, the Companion only asks for one of these. If you are asked for the mirror, it is now turned towards you and you must look steadily into it without hesitation, whatever you may see. If you are asked for the comb, you must boldly reach for it back again and comb the Companion's hair, whatever shape the being may take. If you are asked for the shears, the Companion will offer something for you to cut, and you must shear it without hesitation whatever it may be.

Now the Companion leads you to the crystal bed and as you approach the Sleeper, sorrow wells up again, but this is sorrow for all who suffer, all who will not awaken. Slowly you bend down and gently kiss her upon the lips. [Silent meditation here.]

Out of the silence, from the touch of the Sleeper's lips, comes a vision of what may be when she awakens. Look well upon this vision and remember it. [Short pause here.]

To each of us now comes one of the Seven Companions: their shape seems to change, huge yet small, insubstantial yet strong.

The one that comes to you utters a name, whispering it into your ear. This is the name by which the Companion may be contacted in your future meditations and in sacred places.

Now we are shown a way back, not along the forest path but by a low tunnel revealed to us within the roots of the thorn hedge. This way can only be entered by one person at a time, and to each the journey back to the outer world is different. Remember whatever you see in the low tunnel as you return to the human world, for this is the shortened way back to the presence of the Sleeper. Behind us the presence of the Seven Companions fades, and we find that we are in a familiar place, the place where we began our journey of trials, tests and conscience.

As we return to our outer awareness, let us remember what has occurred in the realm of the Sleeping Maiden. We have been shown a shortened way into her presence; we have learned the name of one of her Seven Companions; we have been tested by the faery warriors and lovers; we have sworn to uphold the sanctity of the land and the living creatures; we have been led by the Lord and Guardian of the forest.

Know that those who have followed, sworn, passed the test and heard the whispered names may take the shortened way. But if you bring others you must travel again by the Moon Pool, the forest and the thorny hedge, until they too have passed through all the encounters.

The Seven Companions

An extract from the original inner teaching on the Sleeping Maiden, from the contact C1.

On your first arrival the Seven Companions will challenge you, and you must tell them what oath you have sworn. Of the Seven three will come to you in turn. One will show you sights in the mirror from which you must not turn away. One will ask for you to comb its hair, and its appearance may be fair or foul. One will offer a thing to you that you must cut instantly with the shears, even if it is precious or dear to you.

On your second arrival three more will come to you, stronger and more wise than the first three. With the same mirror, comb and shears, they will cause wonders that will transform you. For as you saw at first so shall you be seen truly by them, and where you combed at first so shall you be untangled, and where you cut at first without hesitation, so shall you be cut free.

On your third arrival you must treat with the Seventh Companion. Of this nothing can be told beforehand.

The Hall in The Forest

In the next vision we encounter the male Sleeper appearing as a wounded figure in a dying land, showing the Mystery of regeneration.

We see before us, with our inner vision, a flowing stream passing rapidly from right to left. The water is clear and fast-moving, and there are many stones just below the surface. We see that this is a ford or crossing place, and that the stones were laid to make crossing possible for travellers. Each stone is carved with a letter, sign or sigil worn smooth by the passage of the water; the entire bed of the stream shows a strange alphabet cut into the stones. As we look at these letters, shimmering and wavering in the flow or the waters, a large trout swims upstream rapidly and we hear a sudden beating of wings.

Looking up, we find that a heron has landed upon the opposite bank. She is coloured grey, and tilts her head to look at us with her wide staring eye. We meditate briefly upon the meaning of the river, the ford and the watching heron. As we meditate upon the heron, she rises slowly into the air and begins to climb. Our vision flies with her, and it is as if we see with her eyes as she flies over the land.

Beyond the river bank is a winding road leading to a walled city, in which we see a tall castle with shining towers. But the heron turns aside from this place and, flying on, heads towards a distant dark green forest. She flies slowly and steadily, beating her long grey wings; seeing through her eyes, flying with her, we see the trees approaching. First there are the scattered outlying small trees and bushes, and we can see small animals running to and fro in the undergrowth. Many different kinds of birds fly close to the heron as if to challenge her, but they turn away and leave her free to proceed, for the power of the Great Goddess protects her upon this flight.

Now she flies over the green forest, with tall spreading trees reaching into the sunlight. This is one of the ancient great forests, and we can see only the rolling spread of the tree tops, for the branches and foliage are so dense that the ground below is invisible. We can feel a curious heat emanating from the trees as the heron skims their huge crowns, as if the entire domain is a living being radiating vitality. There is a sense of being watched from below, but the heron flies on steadily, heading straight for her unknown destination.

Below us we see a clearing with a herd of deer running swiftly across it, followed by the shadow of the heron made huge in the sunlight. As they move under the tree cover, we catch a short glimpse of a man in a cloak of red leaves, carrying a tall spear. He looks up at us, and we see that he has long flowing red hair and beard, he wears a garland of ivy leaves and berries, and wide spreading antlers grow from his head. In an instant he vanishes from sight, stepping under the trees to follow the deer.

The shape of the land changes now and begins to undulate; low hills covered in trees come into view, and occasionally a hilltop breaks out of the forest. Below we see a bare rocky summit, with a copious spring flowing out to run in streams down into the dense forest below. Many animals come to the spring to drink, and to lick at the red salty earth. We see deer, rabbits, foxes, even a wolf, and then the hilltop is behind us and we fly on.

Now it seems that the heron is looking to right and left, turning and tilting her head, and suddenly we cross a ruined dry-stone wall that seems to stretch across the entire forest, curving gently as if it forms part of a vast circular enclosure so immense that we cannot see its limits. Many of the stones are tumbled and the wall is overgrown with moss and ivy, yet it was once a great work and is still formidable even in decay.

The trees change now, and we find that they are planted in regular rows: looking down, we see that these are short cultivated trees, and that all are withering or dead. We realize that it is a huge dying orchard, with fruit trees decaying and rotting beneath us as we fly. Some are fallen, others are twisted into strange gnarled shapes. Many are bare of leaves, while others are covered in dry brown foliage, as if a sudden frost has hit them and destroyed all life. The heron picks up speed now, as if she knows that she approaches the end of her long flight.

Deep within the dead orchard, we see a large wooden hall, made of massive timbers carved and tinted with many colours. But the vivid gilding and painting has long since been worn away by rain, sun and wind, and the wood shows through in grey weathered patches. Many of the great roof shingles, cut from broad tree planks, are loose or fallen, and dead leaves swirl over the high peak and the proud eagles carved above each gable window.

Now the heron descends, and she lands before the tall doorway of the hall. We see two immense pillars, each cut from the single trunk of a giant tree, and raised up without planing or carving to frame the entrance. Across these trunks, a third huge tree is laid to form a lintel, complete with thick gnarled bark and the stumps of great limbs shorn off. This triple gate of trees was raised up before the hall was built, and the elaborate work of the building was assembled upon its enduring frame.

As we look at the giant doorposts, right and left, each seems to be in the form of a figure, as if the natural shape of the trees resembles a formidable man and woman. Yet when we look closely they seem to be trees again. Now we find ourselves standing before the doorway to that hall within the dying orchard, and the sound of beating wings fades into the distance behind us as the heron flies home to her watching place by the ford.

We look upon the doors of the hall; in contrast to the rough-hewn massive pillars on either side and the rugged trunk of the lintel, they are deeply and ornately carved, set with many metals and crystals. But all is tarnished and weathered as if abandoned long ago. We see image of many stories set into the panels of the door; some we know well, but others involve places, people and creatures that seem to belong to other worlds, other times. Before we can examine these scenes closely, a great gust of wind hurls leaves and twigs against us, and buffets the doors until they open inwards. In the far distance we hear the faint echo of a horn blowing and the blast of wind throws us against the doors. We hurry into the narrow opening, seeking shelter. As we enter within we hear the thundering sound of riders outside; the wind rises to a high roaring gale, and the horn sounds again twice. In the sudden silence which follows, we hear the sound of many creatures gradually approaching; we hear hooves, and wings beating, and we hear footsteps and murmuring faint calls and voices. A great host passes as if following the unseen riders.

The hall within is deep in purple shadow, a rick dark light that tints everything it touches. Now all is silent, and we look about us to see long purple drapes hanging from the high roof beams, filtering the sunlight that shines in through the many tiny windows high above. In this sombre light, we can see a raised platform at the far end of the hall, and we pause before walking towards it.

As we grow accustomed to the quiet, after the howling of the wind and the passage of the riders and their followers, we can hear a faint steady sound of running water. On either side of the great hall, channels are cut in the earthen floor; we see water running bright and clear to our right, while to our left a dark slow-moving stream flows out towards the door. Both streams vanish into deep wells at the foot of the massive door trees, and we hear a very faint sound as if they fall an immense distance into the depths below. We meditate upon this falling sound, and hear many distant echoes and intimations from the mysterious place below that receives the streams . . . [*Short pause here.*]

Now we move towards the platform that fills the far end of the hall: a single ray of sunlight penetrates the shadows and shines briefly upon the platform. We see there a large wide bed, hung about with red and purple drapes; the bed is framed by three posts cut from tree branches; the left-hand post is pure white, the right-hand post is blood red, while the horizontal branch that joins them is a pure emerald green. The ray of sunlight slowly fades, as if obscured by a cloud; we ascend the three steps leading to the platform, and look upon the figure lying on the bed. A great sorrow fills us, for he is deeply wounded.

He is both young and old; his face is fair and his long silver-white hair has grown down over his shoulders. His eyes are closed, and we see no sign of life. He wears a long white robe over silver armour, and an empty scabbard lies by his side. As we approach him, we see that he is breathing very faintly, very slowly. His sides are pierced by a great wound, as if a spear had been thrust through him; we stand before a rent in the robe and armour and flesh that flows with deep red-black blood. From his other side we see a stream of crystal clear water flowing down over the edge of the bed; this double wound is the source of the two streams that pass through the hall and fall away into unknown depths beneath the door trees. We stand in silence, and meditate upon the sleeping knight, his double wound and the terrible sorrow of that place. [*Silent meditation here.*]

As we meditate, we realize that we are not alone in the hall. By the side of the bed we see a huge hound, coloured white with red-tipped ears. It droops its head, and occasionally licks the bloody wound, as if trying to cure the knight in the only way it knows. This hound looks directly at us, and we dare not approach more closely, for it guards the wounded knight.

In the shadows, where the water flows over the edge of the bed, we see a young woman sitting with her head bowed. At first we think she may be weeping, but we can see that she holds a corner of the knight's robe, and has a needle and thread in her hands; the thread shines with faint silver light, and we realize that she is sewing. She is dressed in a black robe edged with gold, and by her side a huge broken sword lies upon the stone platform. We dare not look upon her face, hidden in the heavy purple shadows, yet we know that she is very beautiful and terrible.

We pause to meditate upon the meaning of the hound and the maiden, and a deep silence falls upon the hall. [*Silent pause here terminated by three bell chimes.*] With the chiming of a tiny bell, we hear a wind rising outside, and a clear sunbeam breaks through the gloom from a tiny slit over the distant doorway. It shines the length of the hall onto the head of the bed, where we see a twisted small thorn tree with dry, dead branches.

The sunbeam shines steadily upon the thorn, and the maiden rises and dips the hem of her robe into the stream of water, then walks around the bed, and placing her hand upon the head of the great hound, dips the hem of her robe into the blood. She approaches the thorn tree, and with her back to us, she wrings out the hem of her robe upon it. As she does so, the tree seems to stir and move, and tiny white buds and blossoms break forth from the tips of each branch. The hound stirs and licks his master's terrible wound; the maiden returns to her three-legged stool, and lifts up the knight's robe again. The sunlight fades slowly, and the blossoms close as shadow falls.

We know that it is time to leave, and as we step back from the bed, we see that a rough block of crystalline rock stands at the bed foot. There are faint letters cut into the rock, and we pause to read them before we leave the platform. [*A short pause here.*]

We walk back to the half-open door, and pass out of the hall between the great trees and the deep wells. The sun shines brightly over the dying orchard, and we see that some of the trees still bear healthy leaves and fruit buds. The sight of these trees gives us hope and knowledge of regeneration; we know that the secret lies in the mysteries that we have seen within the hall. As we consider these mysteries, we hear a rushing of wings, and a falcon flies down before us with his harsh cry. He turns his head from side to side, considering us with his bright fierce eyes, and then leaps up into the cloudless sky. Higher and higher he flies, seeming to reach up for the sun itself: we follow the path of his flight until our eyes are blinded by the brightness and we can see no more . . .

Gradually we hear the sound of fast-flowing water, and as our sight recovers, we find that we are standing by a ford over a rushing stream. We stand upon a hard beaten earth track, and know that behind us is the way to the walled city and high castle that we saw when we first met the heron, before our flight into the forest, the orchard, and the purple hall. The secret of a cure for the wounded knight may be taught in that shining place; it is found deep in the wells that receive the blood and water from his wound.

We look across the stream and see a shimmering mist, with a familiar scene beyond it. We wade into the waters, and feel them pull at our legs, but the stones of the ford are firm and give us good footing. As we emerge from the stream, the landscape behind us fades slowly, and even the sound of rushing waters ceases. We find that we are back in the place where we started our journey, and we slowly open our eyes, returning to the outer world. As we do so, we hear faintly the chiming of a bell, and the falling of water into a deep, deep well. Now our journey to the Hall in the Forest is ended.

9. The Divine Child and The Sisterhood

In the first of the two empowered visualizations in this chapter, we experience the awakening of a Sleeper. The most active contact of this type is Merlin, who may appear as a prophet, a wild man of nature, or as a divine child. These aspects are all from the original Merlin tradition, in which the modern stereotype of the wise elder plays only a small part. Merlin is the Sleeper (now awakening) for the land of Britain and for all people ancestrally connected to Britain, but also links to other Northern and Western zones. Behind the figure of the young prophetic Merlin, embedded within it yet the source of it, is the Child of Light. This is the primal male deity of the Underworld, known to the Celts as Mabon, the Son of the Mother. He embodies the spiritual power of regeneration, often identified with the youthful Apollo (a further visualization on the theme is found in Appendix 2). The planetary Sleeper embodying this regenerative power is Christ, and the image of the Child of Light leads into the power of the universal divine child, the ever-becoming.

The visualization is intentionally left open, as you will find your own way to complete it during the periods of silent meditation and communion.

Merlin in The Underworld

The visualization is preceded by entering Silence, and attuning the Seven Directions.

We begin by building in our inner vision the clear image of a room. It is a large square room of balanced proportions. Slowly we look down at the plain wooden floor. Now we begin to look around, and see that three of the walls are plain, with no windows or markings. We realize as we see these walls that they are lit from above, and we look up to the ceiling. From its centre hangs a silver lamp, filling the room with a steady gentle light. Now we turn to see what is behind us, and discover the fourth wall. It is filled completely by a large square mirror. [*Note: you can also set up a room to match this scene, and work within it.*]

Within the mirror we see the room reflected, and in the soft light of the lamp see a softened gentle image of ourselves. As we look upon our own faces they dissolve into shadow, and we know that we must declare our reason for being in this place before the image fades. We have come to seek the chamber of Merlin in the Underworld, starting at the threshold of the four-square room which defines the Seven Directions, Above, Below, East, South, West, North and the Mystery of Within [*see Figure 11 p. 123*].

We face the mirror of the North, and in its depths our own image disappears. At first we cannot see into the mirrors, and cannot focus upon whatever is shown to us. Suddenly the vision clears, and we are standing at the entrance to a long tunnel. Where the frame of the mirror was are two upright stone pillars, with a square lintel overhead. Looking into the tunnel we see row upon row of these stones, leading away into the depths. As the tunnel deepens, the shaped stones give way to natural rock.

Now we approach the mirror and find that we cannot pass through it into the tunnel. As we look within, our ability to see suddenly increases, leaping far down the tunnel. At the very end the tunnel narrows and there we see a face.

At first the face seems faint, almost a trick of the eyes looking into shadow, but it slowly resolves into that of an aged man. His eyes are closed and he seems asleep. His long hair and beard flow out and merge with the rock, and we cannot tell if it is a real man or a carving; one moment he seems human, and the next a being made of stone. His hands and arms rest upon and partly within the stone, and the shape of his body, wearing a long robe, merges with the end wall of the tunnel.

On the floor of the tunnel and set into the stone of the walls we see a collection of simple things. There is a plain brown bowl of wood, a small bronze sword, a plain animal horn bound with cord, and a game board with red, black and white pieces. There are other objects, some difficult to see where they rest in shadow. We look, and pause in silence, meditating upon the aged Merlin and his forgotten treasures, merged into the depths of the land. [*Pause for silent meditation.*]

As we meditate we become aware that there is a subtle change in the air, and a steady draught blows from behind us down the tunnel. Now we must focus our intent upon summoning the sleeping Merlin and bringing him awake, and we know that we must not look round to seek the source of the wind, but let it carry our intent into the depths. Gradually we hear a low note sounding, softly wavering. It seems to come from the far end of the tunnel, and we realize that it is uttered by the horn upon the floor at the feet of the sleeping figure. As we focus upon the horn its sound increases and rises in pitch, until upon its highest harmonic, both sound and wind suddenly stop.

Slowly his eyes open, and the peaceful face comes alive. Behold Merlin awakening from the sleep of Earth, his hands and arms emerge from stone, and as he stands he changes, growing younger. Suddenly the distant waking Merlin comes towards us, and with each step he becomes younger. As he moves a great wind rises from the depths behind him, and we realize that we must stand firm and face into this answering wind blowing from the Underworld.

Merlin rushes towards us, his eyes wide, his face laughing. With the great wind comes light from within the Earth, and Merlin's robe falls away, his silver hair becomes radiant gold, streaming out, his beard fades and vanishes. Now we see a radiant youth, with golden skin and hair glowing with light; he runs to us, and leaps out of the gateway of the mirror. As he leaps we cannot tell if the Child of Light is male or female. With the blast of wind and light we see the treasures that he guarded hurled out and away, and as they pass they too transform. [*Silent meditation here.*]

Note

After a suitable silent period, the group or individual returns to outer awareness. Take note of the visions, impulses, and any other aspects of the experience. If the text is read aloud it becomes an invocation of the Child of Light within the Underworld. You may add a conclusion to the sequence, or may leave it as presented here.

In Appendix 2 there is a further Child of Light visualization, relating to the Underworld Apollo.

We now come to the most powerful induction and vision. Do not try this until you have experienced the others. The simplicity is deceptive as it leads to very deep and specific Underworld contacts, who will subsequently seek to work with you on future projects. Do not enter this realm unless you are totally committed to the quest for planetary vision and awareness.

The Temple of The Four Winds

Meeting the Sisters at the Back of the North Wind

This is a deceptively simple visualization, but within its simplicity is a way towards a very powerful encounter. To make this journey you should be experienced in visualization and visionary travelling, and must have established alliance with a spiritual creature and a faery co-walker. Without these basic Underworld allies and the energy that they mediate, you are unlikely to fulfil your quest at this depth. The allies are also able to help you to return if you have difficulties. You may take the journey alone if you wish, but this is not recommended.

As with all defined or guided visualizations, once you are familiar with the sequence of images and locations you should work without a script, either with a teller speaking (but not reading) aloud or entirely in your own vision. This means learning the material by heart, and such learning is an essential part of the tradition (see *Earth Light* for some detailed guidelines on empowered visualization).

The Journey

Silence is entered.

Dive into the Moon Pool. At the Crossroads meet with your spiritual creature and your co-walker. Take the road to the plain and move swiftly.

Where the road enters the plain an aged thorn tree grows out of a low mound of rocks. This mound is an ancestral chamber tomb, merging into the Earth. It marks the threshold of the great plain of Earth Light and wild fire.

Our intent is to enter the hidden way between the realms, to find the Temple of the Four Winds, and from there to meet with the Sisters at the Back of the North Wind. To do so, we must pass into the ancestral mound. Our spiritual creature goes first into the mound, finding an entrance between the roots of the thorn tree. As

the creature enters, some indwellers may emerge, and we must wait and let them pass. [*Short pause here.*]

Now we see the entrance clearly, and pass into it. Our co-walker comes behind, and we move downwards through a narrow tunnel between stone slabs, bending and sometimes crawling as we follow our creature ally. Whatever the size or shape of our allies, they now change to pass through the descending tunnel. We also feel that we change subtly, as if our bodies mould themselves to the narrow way.

The descent is long, and at last we emerge into a vast cavern, with a high roof and a flat, smooth stone floor. There is a circular stone altar in the centre of the cavern. We are now deep within the body of the land, and see that the way by which we entered is a narrow crack in the cavern wall, running jaggedly into the shadows above. We realize that the cavern floor emits a soft clear light, while the roof is in darkness.

Crossing to the circular altar, we find that it has four arrows cut deeply into it, pointing to each Quarter of the cavern. Yet we cannot tell where each of the Four Directions is, and it feels as if they interchange and fluctuate. This is the Temple of the Four Winds.

Standing at the central altar, we feel the deep silence of this place. [*Short pause here.*] High in each Quarter of the temple, out of reach where the light and shadow merge, we see a dark smooth vent. There are no other entrances or exits except the crack by which we came in, which seems to be the result of an ancient shudder in the Earth.

Now we must affirm our intent to find the hidden sisterhood, said to live at the back of the North wind. In silence we make our intent clear, and as we do so our co-walker moves around the central altar, seeking for the North. Moving to one Quarter of the temple, the co-walker reveals a small door in the wall. This is the North, and suddenly we feel the directions come alive and harmonize with one another. The co-walker changes shape, becoming for a moment one of the huge beings from Falias,[2] and opens the door.

As we pass within we see a symbol scratched lightly upon the door [*see Figure 10*]. Before us is a low tunnel of beaten red earth, and our co-walker goes before us, changing shape again to pass through. As we follow, our spiritual creature comes behind.

The tunnel immediately branches, and branches again, and we are in a maze, a warren of low meandering ways with sinuous curves and many interconnections. Tiny oil lamps give a faint smoky light, barely sufficient to see our way ahead. There is a sense of brooding presence, of a dreaming mind, of the Goddess of the inmost Earth, aware of us wandering in the maze of tunnels. Without the faery ally we would be lost, and we trust in its guidance.

Figure 10 The Door Symbol

Finally we come to a low entrance, leading into a small bare chamber, empty but for a plain table and chair. Neither of our allies will enter this chamber, and after we have crossed the threshold they each move off in a different direction, leaving us alone. [*Short pause here.*]

But we are not alone, for sitting at the table is a small figure in a dark hooded robe. As we see her, the sense of presence intensifies. This is one of the Sisterhood that we have sought to meet, and in silence she communes with us. [*Silent period here.*]

Gradually we are aware that the chamber is empty again, and that we must return to the surface world. At the door we find our allies, and know that they too have met with power in this place. We are led by the faery co-walker back through the maze, and out of the door into the Temple of the Four Winds. As we cross the threshold we hear a deep chiming sound from the tunnel behind, like the boom of a huge gong.

Now our creature ally moves swiftly ahead of us to the crack in the temple wall, and we enter and begin to climb upwards. As we enter there is a blast of sound from the cavern, as a great wind blows through the vents. We climb up, and carry with us something of the power that we have experienced.

Emerging from the ancestral mound we return to the Crossroads, where our allies leave us. Now we walk back to the Moon Pool, and dive through, returning to the upper world.

Note

This sequence should only be undertaken occasionally. Traditionally, it is done in February, the threshold of the year.

Afterword

Both this book and *Earth Light* have been written during a period of great change and unrest across the planet. While many people assumed that a New Age would arise, the death of the old was conveniently overlooked or intentionally ignored. The Underworld tradition ends and begins with the Goddess, whose powers are first of death, then of transformation, and then of rebirth. The ancient Celts (from whom much of the tradition has been inherited) understood that endings must come before beginnings. They marked the cycle of the year from winter to winter, and of the month from dark moon to dark moon, and counted time by nights rather than days. This is not morbidity but wisdom, for it is in the recuperative night that life is transformed and regenerated, ready for the new day in which it will flourish. And it is during the day that life reaches its zenith and begins to decline towards evening.

Even this understanding, that endings come before beginnings, is insufficient, for each cycle, each turning, is mirrored over and over within others. This ceaseless cycle of cycles is our true and fluid state, our interchangeable past and future. At the centre, which is a state of being, is a stillness that very few humans attain. Yet this centrality of being is present in us, in our lands, in the planet itself. If, as seems likely, the New Age has already come upon us and we have failed to recognize it, then we must change.

So far the collective changes have been eruptive, volcanic, destructive. But when we seek to be conscious of the Underworld, we become aware of potential, of the power of *becoming* that is the Power within the Land. I hope that the hints and reinterpretations of tradition that are in this book will attune us, as many as will, to the powers of transformation-out-of-stillness, and liberate us from the rigidity that seeks to endure by stasis.

Work Programme for This Book

1.   Read the entire book from beginning to end as you would a novel. Do not attempt any of the exercises until you have read the book completely, then work in the order suggested below.

2.   Begin the practical work with the basic exercises in Chapter 2: *The Basic Underworld Visualization* (a short simple visualizing sequence for individual practice) and *The Rising Light Below*, an exercise combining physical movement with subtle energies from the Underworld, which integrates your power centres. Do these exercises for a month, one each day, before trying any of the more complex visions. Guidelines for empowered visualization are found in Chapter 2, and in more detail in *Earth Light*. *Earth Light* also contains a work pattern and set of exercises based upon a lunar cycle, which will enhance work with the material in this book.

3.   Work through the long induction narrative in Chapter 2, following the guidelines suggested in the chapter. Aim to make this Underworld journey several times over the next month, until it comes alive for you. Use the *Rising Light Below* exercise after each long visualization to balance your energies. Begin to visit sacred sites or natural power sites and use the basic Underworld entry and exit technique to meditate there.

4.   Work through the practical exercises in Part 2, working with only one exercise each month. You should do the exercise for the month at least once per week, but not daily. Continue working the two basic exercises into your routine, and keep notes.

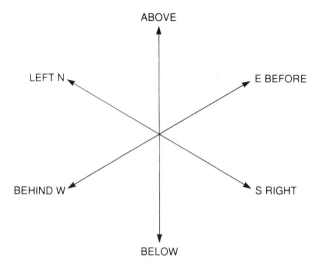

Figure 11a The Seven Directions. *Human*: 1 Above/2 Below/3 Within/4 Before/5 Behind/6 Right/7 Left. *Environmental*: 1 Stars (above)/2 Underworld (below)/3 Land (surface)/4 East/5 South/6 West/7 North.

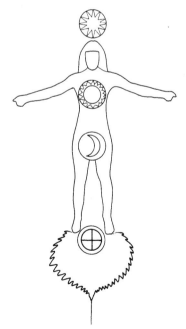

Figure 11b The Rising Light Below

5.   The cycle culminates with the encounter with the *Sisters at the Back of the North Wind*. Do this once only, then pause for at least one week before doing any other inner or meditative work. If your subtle energies are triggered by this encounter, use the *Rising Light Below* to balance them. Remember that this exercise will raise, balance and lower energies, and will alter your awareness of the Underworld forces in general.

Keep notes, particularly of any dreams relating to the Sisterhood or other Underworld themes. After a break of at least one week, you may repeat the induction vision if you wish. After this you would only enter this realm of the Underworld once a year, usually in February or November.

6.   Work with the visualization of Apollo (Appendix 2) before beginning the work cycle again: this one is optional.

7.   Now work through the book again in detail, particularly the inner teachings and direct communications. Make notes and also compare with your own notes made after each exercise or vision.

8.   Begin the cycle again, and by this stage you will have established a set of contacts and working projects. They may not come clear to you for some time, but you will be increasingly aware of Underworld allies and contacts by your second year of work.

9.   Begin to work with some of the suggestions for future developments in Appendix 1.

Appendix 1. Summary of The Underworld Initiation and Suggestions for Future Work

If we summarize the material in this book, it defines a working pattern and some basic methods for pursuing the work successfully. In *Earth Light* and *Power within the Land* combined, we find the following overall sequence:

1. Entering the Underworld and meeting the Dark Goddess. This key experience runs through all Underworld work, underpinning all others.

2. Passing into the Light within the Earth. This is the next constant of the tradition after meeting the Dark Goddess.

3. Revision, reversion and regeneration within the time sequence of the present personality. Leading to:

4. Ancestral and faery encounters. (Remember that 3 and 4 are interactive and may occur in reverse order.)

5. Establishing companions and allies in the Underworld. This may develop as a Triune Alliance.

6. Deeper contacts and awareness of the Three Conditions.

7. Association with hidden orders and temples: this always involves specific training and tasks.

8. Awareness of the Sleepers as follows:

    A. At localities and sacred sites: sacrificial or geomantic localized beings.

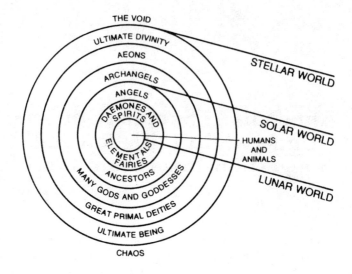

Figure 12 Human and Otherworld Entities

    B.   Within your land or lands: sacred kings, prophets, male and female Sleepers described in myth and tradition.

    C.   Of planetary zones: certain sacred humans merged with god and goddess forms, also the primal deities and primal parents.

    D.   Of the planetary Being: may take form as Mother and Child of Light. Includes the Four Utterances or Fourfold Redeemer (identified in pagan-Christian terms as Lucifer, Adam/Eve, Christ, and Another unknown by any name).

9.   Awakening the Sleepers, usually by working through the Power within the Land and the Triune Alliance. Participating in Underworld patterns of regeneration as you become aware of them.

10.   Intentional mediation between the worlds as a result of all of the above.

When you experience transformative stage 6, you will begin to move out of the use of extended visualizing and into the more direct visionary and energetic/geomantic methods, some of which are outlined in both books. Many people make this crossover at an earlier stage, but it should never be forced or thought of as a grading or merit point. As mentioned before, empowered visualization is an important experience for us as humans whose imaginative faculties have been stunted, but it is only one of the ways forward. In the context of books or other media such as tapes, it is a convenient way of giving form to specific energies and contacts and of communicating that form to as many people as can work with the media.

If you work through all the material in both books, you will eventually develop a future work programme, some of which will come to you from Underworld contacts. Some valuable ideas and methods that are worth working upon are the following:

1.   Using Tarot trump images suitable to the tradition, seek out their hidden Underworld paths (as in Diving through the Moon Pool). Pay particular attention to Moon, Sun, Star, Fortune, Justice, Judgement, Guardian (the *Merlin Tarot*), Death, Tower, and the World.

2.   Entering the Underworld in Triune Alliance at major sacred sites, in cathedrals or abbeys, at natural power locations such as springs, wells, certain trees, and other places which you will eventually sense.

3.   Regularly use the basic Underworld entry method (from *Earth Light*) in a dedicated place indoors and/or outdoors. This is how sacred and empowered locations and gateways are established. Follow this with work with companions and allies, but establish a regular rhythm of basic Underworld opening and entry in its own right.

4.   Work with your sexual partner if he or she is also in the tradition. Seek out a sixfold Alliance pattern.

5.   Study the list of orders on page 23. Work to contact each in turn, through basic entry to the Underworld, the faery realm, or through the deeper visions such as the *Temple of the Four Winds*. Seek out the orders in the South, East, and West of this temple.

6.   Study the folk and faery tales from oral tradition, not

literary reworkings or fantasy literature (such as the basic collections by the Grimm brothers, or in other sources reporting but not embellishing oral tradition). Meditate upon these and find the core visions within them. The visions are more important than any 'meaning'. Do not be surprised if the core visions lead into unexpected realms or contacts; this is often the case.

Appendix 2. Apollo in The Underworld

Opening music: the clear sounds of a simple harp or lyre.

We begin by sitting in silence with our eyes closed, breathing steadily. Within the silence we build an image, seeing it with our inner vision: slowly we enter into a hot summer landscape, with the earth dry and bare. Tiny bushes and aromatic herbs grow out of the rocks that surround us, and we hear small birds piping and singing in the distance.

Directly before us is a steep cliff face, with a narrow passageway leading into a dark cleft in the rocks. The sun beats down, the small birds sing, and we smell the strong perfume of the herbs. There is no other sign of life.

From deep within the cleft in the rocks, we hear a faint sound of music, clear simple notes which seem to come from far below. When they cease, we know that we must enter into this dark chasm, and seek whoever is within. As we approach the rocks, they tower over us and the entrance is narrow: we squeeze painfully through, feeling that the rocks might crush us to death. As we pass within, the heat suddenly vanishes, and we are in the cool shade, with the light of a dark blue sky far above us. As we look up at this light for the last time before plunging into the darkness, we see stars faintly shining, revealed to us by the depth of the chasm filtering the daylight.

Before us now is a jagged cavern mouth, roughly triangular in shape. All is still, silent and waiting. We pass into the cavern, and the light fades almost entirely. For a few moments we stumble upon the stony floor, tripping over rocks, until we feel the walls with our hands and our eyes grow accustomed to the dim grey light. The passageway leads downwards, and as we slowly make our way into the cavern, we feel that the walls are carved with deep spiralling shapes. We long to hear again that strange music to give us confidence in our quest, but there is the deep ancient silence of the rocks and earth, broken only by the faint sound of our own footsteps.

As we reach deeper into the cave, we suddenly hear a faint sliding rasping sound ahead of us, as if some large creature is moving in the shadows. Still touching the walls, feeling the deeply cut spiral patterns, we slowly move forward. We come at last to a point where the passage widens out, and here a screen or curtain is hung across the path. Beside this curtain a torch is burning, set into a cleft in the rock. By its light we see that the walls of the cave are filled with tiny crystals, and that the spiral carving stops just before the curtain, which is of rough wool, dyed in random colours.

All is very still and silent: the torch flickers and gives a dim red light: the woollen curtain, seeming like the rough work of a country loom, sways slightly in the tiny draught caused by the burning torch as it draws air in from far above. In this shadowy torchlit stillness, we feel a strange terror: it begins as a tiny trembling of the feet, and rises up the legs and the spine rapidly. The hair upon our heads bristles, and a cold burning thrills through our flesh. Our heartbeat increases and our eyes water. As this flow of energy passes through us, a tiny mouse suddenly scurries out of a hole by the burning torch, and scuttles up the woollen curtain. When the mouse reaches the top of the curtain, it gnaws through a thread and the entire cloth falls, revealing what is beyond.

Directly before us rears a huge serpent, looking down upon us, and even as we flinch back, it slowly turns turns upon itself and glides off into the depths below. For a moment we are too shocked to move, and then the flowing energy that passes across our skin and through our hair seems to pull us after the serpent. If we seek the Player of the Harp, we must descend into his secret place below.

We step through the thick folds of the rough woollen curtain, and find that the huge serpent has gone before us. Where it has passed the walls are faintly luminous and we follow, uncertain of where it will lead, yet knowing that there are no other passageways or routes to take except to turn and re-ascend, admitting failure in our quest.

The dimly luminous walls reveal tiny crystalline rocks, and streaks of brightly coloured minerals in vivid greens, reds, purples and metallic rainbow hues. Faintly in the depths below, we hear the sound of falling waters, which gradually grows louder as we approach. The sound increases to a constant roar, until we see at last a rushing waterfall that passes like a second curtain over the passageway, falling from the roof above into a deep cleft in the floor. This is lit by a smoking torch, set into a cleft in the rock, and so rapid is the flow of water that it draws the smoke downwards after it.

We cannot see beyond this waterfall, and have no way of knowing how wide the crack in the rock may be. As we pause, uncertain how to proceed beyond the roaring waters, they cease to fall for an instant, and we see far beyond a glow of red light in the distance. Then the waters renew with great force, and we realize that if we are to proceed we must leap through them and trust that we land upon the other side.

So amid the roaring of the falling waters, we draw in a deep breath and run at full speed towards the waterfall: we leap straight through its icy waters, over the deep cleft into the unknown shadows below, and land upon the other side. A smooth tunnel stretches away before us, lit by a red glow that grows brighter as we approach. We feel a steady throbbing deep with the ground, gradually building until it surrounds us, and as we draw near to the light, we find that it is a huge wall of flame rising from the floor of the passageway beneath our feet.

Before this curtain of fire we pause, and in silence make our deepest prayers to the Son of the Mother, whom we seek. [*A silent pause here.*]

As we wait in silence before the curtain of fire, we hear a single note sounding steadily from beyond the flames. Someone strikes upon a string, and the clear vibrant note rings out until the flame curtain quivers. The flames move in resonance with the note, and we see patterns within them rising and falling with the peak and decay of the repeated single tone. Now the hidden musician plays a second note, a high unearthly overtone of the first, and the flames change shape into a regular and beautiful pattern, sculpted by the sound of that overtone. Now the hidden musician plays a higher overtone upon the same string and the flame parts into two, dividing into a perfect vertical lens shape. The edges of this lens stream with patterned fire, swirling and radiating heat and light. As the last resonance of the high overtone fades, we quickly step through the Fire Gate into the unseen place beyond.

We find ourselves in a higher chamber of rock, at the far end of which steam rises from within a pile of rocks. Over the unseen vent from which the steam issues, a tall bronze tripod stands, and upon that a deeply engraved bowl is set. Coiled round the rock, with its head resting by the foot of the tripod, is the giant serpent, which seems to sleep. The fire curtain behind us hisses and crackles, the steam rises, the serpent sleeps. Of the unseen musician there is no sight, nor sound, nor hint.

We see before us a smooth worn area of floor, and one by one sit to wait, looking upon the rising steam and the sleeping serpent. The heady fumes of that deep secret place fill our minds, and visions swim before us. Out of the steam we see a deep black seething cloud, filled with flashes of colour. Into this cloud a single high note is uttered, causing it to part and assume shape. A second note, lower than the first, is uttered, and the shape separates into amorphous clouds. A third note, lower than the second, is uttered, and the clouds explode from within with light. A fourth note is uttered, and the explosions of light begin to move, weaving patterns around one another. A fifth note is uttered and the patterns take shape as stars and planets in the depths of space. A sixth note is uttered, and we look upon one star with its attendant planets, the vision drawing to a planet of blue and green and rolling white colours. The lowest and seventh note is uttered, and we fall towards that planet from a terrible height, and our awareness pauses in stillness, in silence, at the moment of that fall.

[*Here a passage of simple harp music is played, uttering Elemental patterns and tones.*]

We open our eyes to find ourselves in bright sunlight, in a forest glade beside a bubbling spring. Seated upon a rock is a youth with long tangled golden hair. He plays upon a seven-stringed instrument, which seems to change shape as he strikes the strings. He plays with both hands, one hand plucking the strings, and the other touching them lightly to create ghostly harmonics and overtones from within the prime note. As he plays the trees move and leaves burst forth, the spring bubbles and fish leap from its pool, flowers open around his feet. His eyes are of ever-changing colour, each colour shining with a note of the instrument that he plays. Within the surrounding trees many animals are drawn to the glade, and they look upon us without fear.

In the presence of the Son, and the sound of his music, we remain silent. [*Here a silent contemplation is made.*]

During our contemplation an animal or bird has come to each of us, and sits or stands beside us. This creature is the companion allotted to us by the Son of the Mother, the Harper who utters all creation with his music, from stars to crystals, and whose secret sound directs the orders of life and their interaction with one another. We look well upon our companion from another order of life, and when we look up to the rock by the spring, we discover that the Harper has silently departed.

Now the sun begins to set and in the evening light, the trees cast shadows over the sacred glade. One by one the animals and birds depart into the night, and we too must leave and return to our outer world. We feel that our companion creature will be with us on future inner visionary journeys, and remember it well, fixing its image and its qualities in our memories.

Slowly, peacefully, the inner light fades, and we find ourselves sitting in a familiar room. We sit in silent contemplation, and breathe steadily. [*The group makes notes, discusses, or simply disperses in their own time.*]

Appendix 3. The Grail as Bodily Vessel

I

Among the many obscure and fascinating documents relating to the Grail, the diligent reader may find references to two lesser vessels: 'And when our lorde in the dendony was drest, This blode in two cruettes Joseph dyd take' (*The Life of Joseph of Arimathea*); 'Joseph has with him in his sarcophagus two white and silver cruets, filled with the blood and sweat of the Prophet Jesus' (Maelgwyn of Avalon: *Historia de Rebus Britannicus*). We shall return to these curious statements later, as they form part of a persistent oral tradition which manifests to the present day.

The main proposition of this analysis of certain aspects of Grail lore is not, as one might expect, identical to the subject suggested by the title. Before the reader accuses the author of false pretences, and tears the pages from the book, this use of the stump of tradition as a peg upon which to hang the shield of reflection must be explained.

The external appearance of any subject is seldom sufficient to prove its origin and identity, and this is especially true when we examine ancient and obscure traditions, tales, legends, songs and accumulated expositions and commentaries upon such lore. In several portentous and wonderful publications that have appeared amidst loud fanfares in recent years, tradition has been represented as an occult and political conspiracy. The message of the following pages is that tradition is neither a material conspiracy to be unravelled by television documentaries, nor a reliquary of eccentric old gew-gaws, but a catalytic mode of alteration of individual and group awareness. In this respect, tradition may be passive, as the group vehicle of inter-related symbols preserved and passed on through time by various means, or it may be active. The activation occurs through an enlivening of the basic symbols within imagination, a process which we shall refer to again when considering sym-bols from the Grail lore itself.

Any writer who makes such a suggestion stands as a helpless guardian of the entrance to Tophet, the burial place of for-bidden and cursed gods. It was customary for the Hebrews to spit at the very name of this place, which is identical to the Celtic Underworld of Annwn in many respects, the same place in which the Grail may be found. Why helpless? Because the steady stream of pseudo-academic looters that bustles back and forth does not consider such a theory worthy of their spittle; it 'proves' nothing.

The Grail is a vessel of the Underworld, no matter what upper route it has travelled in the hands of exalted intellects. Qabalists may understand this paradox instantly, but it will be more difficult for orthodox Christians or those who follow Eastern paths adapted for the use of Westerners.

Familiarity with the source material is essential, and the suggestions offered are meaningless unless related to the early and basic 'Grail' texts, or other sources mentioned in context. The main source is *The Quest of The Holy Grail* (translated by P. Matarasso, Penguin, 1976). No amount of retrospective com-mentary can replace the actual legends themselves; they are the vehicle of a living, powerful and ultimately undeniable inner transformation. As tradition implies, this transformation fer-ments from within to express itself outwardly, and not in any mere political or religious or ephemeral form.[1]

One of the hallmarks of a great symbol, such as the Grail, is that it may manifest in a number of different ways to human perception, yet each manifestation will be attuned to the nature of the original. Such a definition is not identical to suggestions that the Grail is 'all things to all men' or that it may be 'what-ever we wish it to be'. A great symbol or key to altered awareness has limits, even if we cannot perceive them, and we may presume that the Grail is no exception to this rule.

The activation of a great symbol, or arch-symbol, can cause numerous effects within apparent serial time, all of which are analogous to their original, albeit with different modes of expression. The relationship between such manifestations cannot be deduced by mere lists of their correspondences, but by a deep realization that they are simultaneous expressions of one original model.

Careful consideration of this process suggests that whereas the ramifications of a great symbol may indeed be countless in expression, no one of these units alone can be true to the original. To be defined by material expression involves limitation, but we should not blandly assume that if we patch all the limited expressions together the resulting whole will be a sum of all parts! When this mechanical approach to symbolism is attempted, the potency and clarity of the original is inevitably lost.

Paradoxically, perhaps, it is one of the major operational laws of magic that the whole may operate through one part, even though the total accretion of parts can never make the whole. Understanding of this simultaneous diversity in unity was common to the philosophy, metaphysics and ritual of the ancients; it is currently undergoing a considerable intellectual revival.

The pagan and early Christian symbolists were eminently practical. They expected, even demanded, that their most potent symbols should manifest through the physical body. It is in this context that we shall consider the Grail, always bearing in mind that its manifestation as a bodily vessel, a human being, is identical in essence (but not in mode of expression) to manifestation in any other consensual form.

The most dramatic and far-reaching religious variant of this potent manifestation may be found within orthodox Christianity, modulated through the individual preference for cult expressions of the primary original faith. The Christian Incarnation was founded upon a well-known and widespread system of magic, available not only to so-called 'initiates' but also to everyday common folk.

While adherents of esoteric Christianity will dispute that the Incarnation was of a higher order or degree than those of similar pagan rituals, they cannot reasonably suggest that the symbolism of virgin birth was not of long standing and well established before, during and after the appearance of the Saviour. Orthodox religion, of course, does not allow such considerations at any price, even in the light of factual historical evidence such as classical literature, archaeological proof or comparative religion and mythology.

Of particular interest in our present context is the repeated evidence that such an ancient system may still operate today, or rather that people believe that it still operates. Whether or not such a system is in any way effective or valid for the twentieth century is a separate discussion.

Within the popular revival of interest in ancient and racial lore, a revival which occurs with almost every generation, acceptance of the Grail as a Celtic and early Christian symbol has become commonplace. Despite the ever-increasing mass of literature that examines the manuscript and folklore evidence relating to the subject, there are several curious aspects of what might be termed 'Grail lore' that spill over into British tradition, and these should be considered within the broader context of magical practices and both pagan and Christian symbology.

While our analysis will revolve around one brief and specific tradition, it will not be limited to that subject alone, and will not adopt the typical approach of literary comparison, or semi-scientific folklore. Much of the material offered will probably be familiar to the reader, but some of the conclusions may be startling.

The tradition from which we begin is pleasantly short, appearing in literary form early in the thirteenth century, in the work of Robert de Boron. The reference, to two vessels or 'cruets' associated with the Grail, is a feature of the familiar tale of Joseph of Arimathea, and his association with the holy ground of Glastonbury. The endless argument about the origins and validity of this material is well known, but the absorption within popular and esoteric tradition is worthy of close examination. (*Joseph d'Arimathie*, Robert de Boron, c. 1200.)

No better way can be found to emasculate old traditions than to find a 'proof' of their origins. What is seldom grasped by the pernicious peddlers of 'proof' is that many apparently fabricated traditions find their way into the common imagination, and are openly accepted for centuries after the originators (or presumed originators) are dust.

Before proceeding any further, we must make clear to the reader that we have no intention of 'proving' anything. It is unnecessary to prove traditional lore; if it could be proven it would be valueless. We are concerned only with the undeniable fact that a tradition exists, and that the many branches of that tradition (literary, folklore and esoteric) all offer similar information, though in confused and fragmented forms.

To treat such material as a mere detective problem, to suggest that there were or are actual secret 'orders' preserving lore into the present era for purposes of world domination, is to utterly degrade the value of traditional lore, and effectively reveals the petty mentality of the authors of such theories.

One cannot 'own' the Grail; nor can one 'prove' a Tradition.

Sources for the pattern of tradition under analysis are numerous, and references may be found within:

1.   orthodox Christian teaching and scripture. Old and New Testaments;
2.   pagan parallels to Christian mythology;
3.   folklore parallels, in native British and European tales, songs, ballads and games or ritual dramas;
4.   the main body of Grail literature from the twelfth and thirteenth centuries, which offers heretical Christian and pagan traditions in profusion;
5.   esoteric traditions, as taught in European and British schools or systems of magic. These include the so-called 'inner-plane' teachings, devolving from sources not of this world, but are well represented in oral teaching, ranging from revived witchcraft through to various forms of Qabalah.

Once again we should state, at the risk of being repetitive, that the following pages are not offered as a 'proof' of anything whatsoever; nor do they necessarily constitute a statement of belief or practice on the part of the author. The true value of esoteric or symbolic lore is not found within its content, but through the effect of that content upon awareness.

Setting aside the matter of social or historical, or even literary, validity, we must consider the power of traditional material to shape and develop individual and group consciousness. In certain cases, that power acts suddenly, dynamically and irrevocably.

Eastern systems of altered consciousness have gained considerable attention, and the use of certain tales and sayings, such as the famous Zen 'koan', are now well known. Keys of this sort work by jolting the awareness of the individual into new and previously unexperienced modes. This catalytic power may be experienced to very deep levels through the Mystery of the Grail.

Within the overall Mystery, there are a number of lesser but significant mysteries which devolve from it, which we might call sub-symbols. Such sub-symbols are useful means of approach to the greater symbol, and often act as short-cuts or secret ways to understanding, bypassing corrupted or authoritarian routes.

It is within such a context that we should consider the esoteric traditions that suggest possible physical descendants of Jesus Christ. Such traditions are not required to be factual, though they may very well be so, and are utterly prostituted when treated as seamy press scandals.

They are, in fact, operative as 'koans' or as parables. The realization of a traditional genetic inheritance, a magically acti-vated bloodline, was intended to shock the awareness of the initiate into new modes or realms of reality. The initial jolt may have been great indeed, in the face of stultifying orthodoxy, but the process of association and absorption resulting from the first shock attunes to a level of awareness that runs under religious propaganda, and provides a continuing tradition.

More significant, from a practical approach, is that the potent catalysing effect is not triggered by mere verbal or literary analysis; it comes as a surprising and inward certainty, through participation in the symbolic language of the Grail Mystery. To this end, popular works aimed at earning money from bowdlerizing tradition and esoteric keys may not, in fact, do as much damage as one thinks.

During previous centuries, however, the realizations under discussion were regarded as secrets, not in themselves, but in their linking or bridging function between esoteric practices and the mass, group or racial consciousness. These secrets, which were punishable heresy to preach, were regarded as games, jokes and silly tales. The myth-historian Geoffrey of Monmouth, for example, went to great lengths to tell us re-peatedly that his material was full of puns, even at the risk of being accused of mocking his noble patrons. The Grail legends, however serious in their intent, contain this same childlike accumulation of traditional lore.

The precedents for such an approach are ancient indeed, and are firmly stated in Luke XVIII: verse 17. 'Verily I say unto you, Whosoever shall not receive the kingdom of God as a little child shall in no wise enter therein.'

While there is no firm evidence of coherent or secret teaching being perpetuated through the centuries, there is evidence of a recurring tradition which is protean and indestructible. From a magical standpoint, and even from the grossly materialist suppositions of modern psychology, we find that lore connected to 'genetic magic' arises spontaneously through contact, real or imagined, with certain branches of the Western Mysteries.

It is lore of this sort that advises that the 'cruets' mentioned by de Boron were offspring of Jesus of Nazareth; male and female vessels of seed and blood. In both orthodox and esoteric symbolism, 'water' is a euphemism for seed or semen in certain contexts.

This esoteric tradition may be communicated by word of mouth, and may also occur as a 'communication' from non-physical entities, who teach a coherent and applicable body of lore combining pagan and Christian enlightenment within a physical Mystery framework, aimed at manifestation through human reproduction and reincarnation.

The validity of this teaching is of no importance, but its repeated occurrence within individual and group awareness even to the present day is of great significance. It shows the operation of certain symbolic modes of consciousness through the interpretation of the emotions and the intellect into physical expression.

This same 'mystery' has occurred for thousands of years, and has many variant expressions in the main body of Grail lore. It may be fashionable from time to time to 'prove' that the mystery has been faked or forged, or that it is real and exists through the occult activity of secret organizations. The truth may be more simple, rooted in the regeneration of such concepts within group awareness. That which does not regenerate is not the Grail.

The European development of symbolism expressing a vessel of regeneration may be traced to famous manuscript references, reporting ancient Celtic tradition. These in turn compare favourably with classical references, and with remains from the Roman-Celtic period as early as the first century AD. Sites such as Aquae Sulis, with its Celtic-Roman temple of Sul Minerva, offer practical working models of pagan belief in regeneration within the Underworld or Otherworld.

This regeneration motif is present in folklore and folksong collected from oral tradition during the twentieth century, though references are widely diffused, and the word 'grail' never occurs.

The heretical Grail lore of the twelfth and thirteenth centuries binds pagan and early Christian beliefs with a strong thread of monastic influence in interpretation. This interpretation, which is not always orthodox, acts as a cement that enabled the pagan and rather 'dangerous' native lore to hold together. Whereas in the work of Geoffrey of Monmouth, the various mythical traditions were combined upon an old 'after the cataclysm' model, in *The Quest Of the Holy Grail* such traditions are linked by a 'redemption of the world' model.

We know from sources which noted Welsh lore in the Middle Ages that the Celts believed in a Cauldron of Immortality. This vessel restored dead men to life, though they were sometimes dumb, and renewed pork joints from old bones. It was part of the sacred feast of the dead ancestors, and was employed in a ritual which was aimed at conferring divine knowledge and immortality. This theme was also found in Greek mythology and ritual.

The magical vessel had its home underground, and all wells, springs and lakes were regarded as Gateways to the Underworld. A much-quoted Welsh poem, *Preiddeu Annwn*, records a magical raid upon the Underworld by a band of heroes and this theme of theft from the depths recurs in various forms throughout folklore, magic and religion. The poem is likely to be an early example of the Grail quest.

The foundation of belief in a vessel of power, and its place in the Underworld lay in the pagan concept of exchange between the human and otherworlds, a concept still important in ritual magic today. Duality of death and life was unknown, they were manifestations of one power, not entities in conflict.

A most obvious vessel for magical power in the outerworld is the human being, and this is reflected in the constant belief in exchange found in period inscriptions from the Celtic-Roman culture, and from classical accounts of the Celtic attitude to physical death. Humankind bargained with the Underworld.

It is in this context of exchange and interplay between human and otherworld powers that practices of human sacrifice arose. Such practices were inseparable from systems of controlled birth or potential reincarnation.

Although this system is generally bandied about in modern works on magic, and much of the material concerned is vague and nonsensical, there is a strong suggestion of its continuity in esoteric traditions and in folk or rural magical practices. The modern revival of witchcraft, although essential and praise-worthy in its attempts to recapture a fresh relationship with nature powers, has tended to cloud perception of the magical systems concerned by claiming traditions without recourse to the metaphysics which underpinned their operation. While the Christians attempted to use the conceptual models of the ancients without allowing the generative magic that gave such models life, the modern pagans have picked up the cast-off generative organs without considering that they are fallen from a great and divine body of wisdom. Little wonder, in the face of such a conflict, that the prototype of the Maimed Fisher King should have been pierced through the thighs, losing his ability to reproduce. This type of symbolism refers not only to spiritual imbalance or sickness, but to actual physical illness and repro-ductive processes.

In its simplest form, we have a story of heroes who raid the mysterious otherworld to gain a great prize; in its most com-plex form we have the quest for the Grail. In both cases, there is a powerful motif connected with fertility; not fertility in a merely sexual reproductive sense, but a through line of fertility, reaching from the Underworld, to the physical body, to the mental, emotional, and spiritual fertility of the individual and of the tribe or race.

That which does not regenerate is not the Grail.

Celtic practices of ancestor worship (the cult of the dead) involved the spirit passing into the otherworld or Underworld, and then communicating with a seer or seeress who still lived in the outer or human world. This system was so widespread in the ancient cultures that it merely needs to be mentioned here, as the reader will have access to numerous works which speculate upon it in great detail. The esoteric practices of con-trolled fertility and timed conception were aimed at specific reincarnations of certain ancestors. Over a considerable period of time, a theoretical reservoir of illuminated souls became available to the mysteries which operated in this manner. It was believed that any particular king was literally the vehicle of all his ancestors, and this is reflected in examples from Irish tradition.

The widespread pre-Christian system, often called the rituals of the sacred king in modern literature, permeated through orthodox religion well into historical time, and much of its subtle practical operation is enshrined in the Grail legends.

This enshrinement takes two forms; as specific, almost offhand examples of apparently unrelated incidents, and as a continual theme reflecting upon the value of divinely given qualities of nobility.

We should not be surprised, therefore, when one branch of this material suggests that actual children were born to Jesus of Nazareth, and that they should be of the blood of the dark myth-woman of Christianity, Mary Magdalene.

The type of tradition outlined may be horribly unorthodox in the crude authoritarian sense, yet it harmonizes with some deep and persistent myth that is rooted in the group conscious-ness expressed within the Western Mysteries. The physical vessel of the body is also the spiritual vessel of renewal, either in the timeless experience of inspiration, or through numerous reincarnations, depending upon the will, beliefs and culture of the individual.

In Celtic imagination, there is little to separate the dead, the ancestors, the faeries or otherworld powers, and those about to be born. Similar beliefs were held by many pagan cultures, often refined to great sophistication and complexity.

All such arbitrary selection of lore might indeed be regarded as superficial, were it not for several undeniable facts that sup-port our curious conclusions, without ever proving them. The most important indication is the persistence of certain themes both in and out of manuscript or print, particularly as folklore or as esoteric teachings, maintained by oral traditions.

The second significant element is the relatively modern science of genetics. Knowledge of this field may have been applied by the ancients, but based upon a rather different primary model to that of deductive and experimental science.

If we dare to encapsulate this complex subject, we might define genetics as one of the major factors in the construct that appears as a 'human being'. Genetics form one of the matrices that enable the entity to operate through many levels of func-tion in manifestation. Specialists are still researching the rela-tive values of genetics, environment, conditioning, innate response and so forth, but the genetic inheritance is as proven as any workable scientific theory, and new applications are constantly being discovered for genetic theories.

In short, science instructs us that we inherit something of our ancestors, as was common knowledge to the ancestors them-selves. Such a concept is central to the practice of ritual magic;

orthodox authority was able to charge pagans and heretics with necromancy. Geoffrey of Monmouth tells us that the British King Bladud 'spread necromancy throughout the land', which is merely another way of saying that his forefathers were ancestor worshippers. Both archaeology and classical sources confirm Geoffrey's statement.

The Celtic lore in Geoffrey is only superficially concealed, and the reader will find many parallels to the later Grail legends in *The History of the British Kings* (translated by Aaron Thompson, 1718, or the more modern translations, such as that of Sebastian Evans). While Geoffrey used to be popular as a 'source' for the Grail legends, as his work 'predated their appearance', scholars now suggest that all such material may be derived from general sources within oral lore . . . a concept which has always been understood by teachers of esoteric traditions, and by modern folklorists.

It is significant that Geoffrey applies a genealogical proof to his post-cataclysm mythical history.

How is the genetic inheritance communicated? Through the interaction of male and female characteristics. In magical language these factors have long been expressed as The Seed and The Blood. The Celtic obsession with genealogy is not entirely a claim for social superiority. In the not too distant past, it was the equivalent of the modern genetic chart; a statement of direction with respect to the future, confirmed by the records of the past.

Readers who are familiar with the Christian Bible will remember the two distinct genealogies offered for Jesus Christ, by Matthew and Luke, in their opening chapters. Matthew gives an orthodox male line of inheritance, whereas Luke shows a female line, including miraculous births of both Jesus and John the Baptist brought about by the mediation of the Archangel Gabriel upon the 'daughters of Aaron', Elisabeth and Mary.

In many ancient cultures, the matrilinear line is primary in the definition of race, tribe, inheritance of property and other matters, and this emphasis is found in a great deal of Celtic folklore. Although modern revivalist pagans often take this, perhaps rightly, as evidence of a once dominant Goddess culture, it also reflects the magical and metaphysical concern with genetic lines.

Many of the clearly emphasized incidents within the Grail

cycle involving female lines of descent, blood and mysterious conceptions should be analysed in the light of modern genetic science. They are likely to be a magical analogy or operative model which uses a different vocabulary, but relates to the same processes as the modern expositions. This comparison should not be taken too literally, however, for the magical or metaphysical models were concerned only with the inheritance of otherworld power through the physical body, and were based upon long cycles of observation and correlation linked to seership. These are the very cycles that are referred to in both genealogies of Jesus, and which appear again the replication of Christ in the form of Galahad.

The special role of Jesus in replacing the hero who raids the otherworld is emphasized in several ways in Celtic Christian mythology, the earliest form of Christianity native to Britain.

Scottish Highlanders retained the ancient tradition that Jesus was fostered by the native goddess Brigit, the most powerful beneficial goddess of the Celtic pantheon. In early social structures, the foster mother and midwife were as important as the blood mother; in magical terms that which brings a child from the womb will powerfully affect the outer life of that child. The birth of the Saviour was associated with the blessing of the most important culture goddess of the pagan world, Brigit to the Celts, and Minerva to the Romans, patroness of so many heroes who plundered the dark powers of the Underworld, slew monsters and brought special aid to their people.

As a result of this significant midwifery, which may be interpreted in several ways, Jesus fulfilled his expected duty by the so-called Harrowing of Hell – his journey through the Underworld. It would have been unthinkable that such a divine hero might pass from the outer world without reproducing his line; the blood line caries the message of the experience of his role as Mediator and Saviour. The power is passed *directly* through the body, bypassing all other mental and emotional routes.

It is not surprising that this heretical aspect of early Christian belief should be rigorously suppressed – the aim of the later church was to control and suppress the power, not to scatter it broadcast as a universal seed. Esoteric tradition advises us that sensuality may be a snare, but that specific reproduction along certain special lines may be beneficial to us all. Concepts of this sort are subject to considerable abuse, and historic manifestations up to and including the present century have frequently been of the worst possible nature. The abuse comes through literal attempts to 'prove' the system by 'purifying' human groups, a quite absurd and impossible venture, which utterly ignores the complex time-scales inherent in magical work, and wilfully rejects the spirit of true grace and enlightenment which blows where it will.

Despite the obvious abuses, against which we might choose to weigh the appalling career of the orthodox churches in their abuse of humanity at large, we may indulge in a few (idle) speculations. If Jesus of Nazareth had been initiated in the ancient mysteries, or as an Essene, or during his traditionally avowed youth in Druid Glastonbury, he would have had a clear understanding of the magical lore of sacred breeding and reincarnation. Indeed, the fragments of the suppressed Gnostic gospels suggest that he tried to apply this knowledge in rather specific ways which aimed at removing the enlightened from the physical matrix of consensual reality through the practice of magical chastity. We will return to this disappearing act shortly, in later and lesser variants.

It might not be too wildly imaginative to suggest that there could be no better way of perpetuating a spiritual revolution in a fallen world than to plant its seed within the blood of following generations. Such is the esoteric tradition which deals with the two Vessels or Cruets associated with the Grail.

II

It is difficult for the retrospective analyst of folklore or of period embodiments of tradition in manuscript to decide exactly what the true nature of the subject matter may be. This is why we gain such endless occupation in the study of early literature and of oral tales and songs.

Material may be classified into units of local, national and even international currency as motifs, but this does little more than show a crude statistical summary, a preliminary organization which tidies up the sweepings ready for real examination.

Ultimately it is the personal belief of the student of any school or body of lore that enlivens and colours interpretation. Some modern writers regard all ancient lore as nothing more nor less than the inevitable product of economic and social struggles; many folklorists insist that apparent evidence of early magical or pagan lore in modern folk sources is either an illusion on the part of the interpreter, or an intrusion culled from nasty literature. Regrettably, they are often correct in their insistence.

During our analysis, we have made the monstrous presumption that a great deal of ancient matter is incorporated within oral tradition and that this matter is available to the present day, in numerous though attenuated forms. We have capped this presumption with an even greater one; that a careful comparison of standard folklore and song, magical symbolism and pagan philosophy will reveal many practical insights into the Grail legends.

Any student of magic who reaches beyond the superficial levels so profusely available in publication will have realized that magic is somehow concerned with 'genetics'. Our ancestors, from whom we inherit our magic as well as our physical characteristics, were most concerned to perpetuate certain blood lines that held special abilities. If the Grail legends are considered in this light, they are found to be replete with indications of genetic magic, especially aimed at spiritual regeneration attuned to physical regeneration.

As we mentioned above, *The History of The Kings of Britain* assembled traditional magical and religious motifs upon a mythical 'post-cataclysm' framework, a rationalization of myth in the classical form of the fall of Troy, and the flight of a band of heroes. The Grail legends, on the other hand, deal with the Fall and Redemption. By the time alchemical works had begun to appear, based upon the common symbolism found within the Grail and pagan lore, and later refined by the great hermetic philosophers of the fifteenth, sixteenth and seventeenth centuries, the esoteric tradition as a whole had begun to concern itself with the redemption and regeneration or restoration of the Fallen World. It is in this atmosphere that the monumental works of Christian metaphysics allied to magical practices appeared. The perceptive reader may detect a similar cycle, expressed in different modes, from the eighteenth century to the present day, distributing the three phases over a shorter time scale.

A few obvious examples of genetic magic within the 'Quest' would be:

1. Lancelot, whose excellence is the product of his breeding

and not of his own inward efforts. He falls into sin and despair through the squandering of his natural gifts, and suffers considerable hardship before he attempts to develop his spiritual essence or true nature and attune his physical inheritance and prowess to its proper end. A believer in reincarnation might suggest that Lancelot lives off the capital of previous lives, without fully becoming aware of his function in the present life. He is, in this sense, an example of everyman, though a highly amplified and noble example in many respects.

2.   Galahad, the product of a mysterious liaison between Lancelot and a maiden. Galahad seems to be a model of perfection, so much so that his father asks why he does not aid him in his spiritual plight.

The esoteric answer to this question is that if Lancelot and Galahad are to become spiritually free, each to his own degree, then they must transcend the old genetic cycles of magical work, and realize a truly spiritual inspiration.

3.   Arthur, the offspring of a union arranged by magical illusion, and traditionally said to be under the protection of the enchanter Merlin during his childhood.

Most important of all, however, is the master model that explains many of the lesser examples and characters in the Grail legends, so we will move straight to this without listing further individuals, especially as such lines may be found clearly stated within the 'Quest' itself.

The major key is, of course, the tale of the 'Tree of Life', which clearly offers the salvation of humankind through the action of the power of woman. This tale should be studied in detail, and compared to topological models such as the Qabalistic Tree of Life, a mathematical structure which shows the interrelationship between metaphysics and human energies through various conceptual worlds. It also shows the pattern of genetics and relationships which have been 'discovered' by modern science and psychology.

Of particular relevance to our suggestion that the Grail may manifest as ancestor worship or necromancy is the action of Solomon in the legend of 'The Tree of Life'. Through meditation upon the quality of womanhood, Solomon, the model or archetype of wisdom, achieves the revelation that 'there shall come a woman through whom man shall know joy greater an hundred times than is your sorrow; and she shall be born of your inheritance.'[2]

Delighted by this knowledge, Solomon studies 'every sign according him, whether waking or in dream, in the hope of coming at the truth of the ending of his line'.

Finally, having discovered that The Virgin shall be his descendant, and that the last male of his line shall be even more valorous than Josiah, he decides to send a message through time to his descendants.

The resulting magical ship, needless to say, is devised by his scheming wife, who uses the three sports of the Tree of Life in its symbolism; Red, White and Green. While the male struggles to send his knowledge through time, the female provides the means whereby this might be realized, and a third and mysterious power activates the vessel and casts it off upon the ocean of life.

The entire venture is a simple restatement of the Celtic application of ancestor lore, magical genetics and divination; science-arts which were held in common by the advanced peoples of the ancient world, and which persist to the present day in diffused forms.

One factor which is easily overlooked in consideration of the Grail legends is that their originals were from an oral tradition; the reader of, or rather the listener to, the Grail stories would have been comfortably able to relate their content to a large store of similar tales, songs and entertainments which were widespread in all levels of society.

It is only in relatively recent years that an understanding of folklore has enabled scholars to realize the nature of the Grail material; it is combined and edited from a common stock of lore, and doubtless contains innumerable cross-references, themes and motifs which the modern reader cannot glimpse, or which have been lost.

Such themes, however, cannot be 'traced to originals', for they are the currency of communication in the dreamlike process of the group imagination. It cannot be over-emphasized that Grail lore was intentionally fused from parts in common regular use in the general imagination; it cannot be denied that this fusion created a new and powerful imaginative entity that works as a vehicle for transformation when activated. The works of Homer are directly comparable.

In modern jargon, we could suggest that the Grail legends, and the related works such as *The History of The Kings of Britain* and *The Prophecies of Merlin*, are models of the racial psychology; but they are also maps of the magical physiology of the relationship between the Ancestors, the Land and the Underworld.

Primitive examples of this type of symbolism were operative as rituals during the early part of the twentieth century, and a few still persist today. A list of such examples from folklore would be long indeed, but one of the most famous examples, 'The Cutty Wren', involves a ritual hunt for a mythical bird (represented by a real wren) and its cooking in 'a bloody great brass cauldron'. The remains are so large that the poor can be fed with the spare ribs alone.

Promoters of the theory of sacrificial kingship often use this folksong and ritual as proof of survival, but setting such a complex argument aside, we can observe identical motifs to those of the raid upon the Underworld in the poem *Preiddeu Annwn* mentioned above. For while the gap in time between the two is many centuries, the message has been sent down through time in the vessel of the common tradition.

The genetic flow, or pattern of communication with the ancestors in the otherworld, is intimately linked to the persistence of a common tradition which expresses itself in song, story and ritual, carrying material that appears to be retained from ancient cultural and magical sources. We would emphasize the apparent or superficial nature of this similarity, which is more likely to be the result of a deeply regenerative power of group consciousness than of active preservation and policy.

The legend of the 'Tree of Life' also gives an insight into the nature of magical or spiritual virginity, an esoteric understanding which greatly pre-dates the Christian emphasis of its appearance in the Grail lore. Maidenhood, we are advised, is a mere physical circumstance, but virginity is a state of awareness, a mode of consciousness. The collator of the Grail stories is intentionally stating a central and powerful magical law – something which must be fully realized before any type of magical work becomes truly effective. It has very little to do with morality and physical chastity, and a 'virgin' in ancient terminology need not be a 'maiden'. This applies equally to males and females, as the Grail legends repeatedly state.

Virginity is a primal or spiritual state, whereas maidenhood is the physical mirror of that state, which occurs through renewal of the body in reincarnation. Conversely, a maiden may not be virgin, but maidens who are not virgin are of little use in magic, contrary to popular opinion and fiction.

This metaphysical law was clearly stated by Jesus: 'But I say unto you, that every one that looketh upon a woman to lust after her hath committed adultery with her already in his heart' (Matthew V: verse 28). Regrettably, subtle magical laws of this sort have been deliberately poisoned and misrepresented, leaving modern men and women with a dismal heritage of separation from their true power of relationship.

When we are advised that both the mother of Jesus and the mother of John the Baptist were 'the daughters of Aaron' and conceived as virgins, we are experiencing a mythical reworking of the magical rituals common to the pagans, whereby special breeding was aimed at bringing forth certain powerful ancestral or otherworld beings by the purity of the male and female partners, synchronized to specific times and places. Such a suggestion, however, in no way challenges or lessens the religious or spiritual power of the Virgin, as She is the essence, the Virgin of all virgins, and the human manifestation of the Grail.

With this point, we have come full circle in our argument, and repeat that a great symbol, such as the Holy Grail, may manifest in several different modes simultaneously. The difference is actually in the perception or level of consciousness of the recipient, as is clearly shown at the conclusion of the 'Quest'.

Although we have found a convenient circularity in the exposition, it does not suggest that all Mysteries are identical in operation or results, even if they use identical methods and key symbols. In the case of 'genetic magic', esoteric tradition supposes several sources for magical lines of descent, initiation and communication from otherworld beings. These vary from widely published (but little understood) sources such as the lost continent of Atlantis, to quite obscure individuals with utterly localized traditions. Royal and noble families are often included, though pedigree is no guarantee of magical and spiritual power. As a mere aside, the perceptive student of history will have realized that most, if not all, of the ancient European blood lines have been usurped.

To express the matter crudely, not all members of the Mysteries are descendants of Jesus Christ, but there is a symbolic tradition that implies that any one of them *might be*. The corollary, that any one of us might be a descendant of some lesser divine hero or sacred king, is almost equally important.

It is this imaginative potential that acts as the super-catalyst to fire the consciousness into new realms, and the resulting changes will be shaped by the matrix which contains the imaginative energies at the moment of transition or translation. This method is radically different from the standard concepts of prayer, faith or even of meditation, and is one of the true magical or esoteric 'secrets' handed down to us by our native tradition. An understanding of this pattern of human consciousness, this method of transformation, enabled the early Christian authorities to sink certain programmes of control very deeply into the group mind, by tapping the collective symbols and merely reconnecting them in a slightly, but deliberately, confused manner.

If, as genetic science informs us, there is a set of coordinates that defines the physical entity derived from our ancestors; if, as modern psychology suggests by vaguely plagiarizing the philosophy of the ancients, there is a deep fund of group or racial memory, how may we awaken this knowledge, wisdom and understanding, locked within our very cells and our hidden depths of consciousness? Might not the deep memories and the bodily pattern be one and the same thing?

Magical tradition avers that this is indeed the case, and offers a full and effective method for such an arousal.

Folk tradition supports this with accounts of certain persons who made trips to the otherworld while still in bodily form. Some of these returned as seers or seeresses, while others remain lost but not dead. One typical example of this class of magical disappearance is the Reverend Robert Kirk of Aberfoyle (1644–?), the first translator of the Bible into Gaelic, and collector of an early set of examples of faery lore and the Second Sight. People were still attempting to rescue Kirk from faeryland only a generation ago, as the result of a local tradition that had continued for almost 300 years.

Religious tradition offers us the example of Enoch, who walked with God and 'was not', and, more relevant to the Grail, the Roman Catholic belief in the physical ascent of the Virgin into Heaven.

Similar examples might be enumerated at great length, but their significance in our present context is that the belief was attached to historical persons, such as Kirk, Thomas of of Ercle-doune, and others within British or Celtic tradition. It is this demanding of literal physical manifestation (or perhaps we should say un-manifestation) that is close to the inmost heart of Western magic; this same deep intuition that the divine powers must flow through the body has led to popular misconceptions of the work of the alchemists, magicians and metaphysicians of past centuries. More subtly, it leads to the common complaint against 'magic', that the art does not work, for the experimenter had no physical results to be observed or experienced.

The demand that magic work upon the outer matrix or physi-cal world is no mere puerile materialist plea: it runs ancient and deep, and is actually the result of our most potent collective intuition about apparent reality; that it can be changed.

Firm attempts to combine magical power, blood lines and temporal power have frequently appeared in history, such as the foundation of the Order of the Garter, based upon Grail symbolism. Such organizations, dependent upon hierarchies of beings similar to those of the orthodox church, inevitably fail.

The true value of such traditions as those outlined briefly above lies in a full absorption of the symbolism, and its subse-quent activation to create a revolutionary alteration of aware-ness. This revolution is not limited to politics, religion or even personal mental activity, but runs through each and every aspect of the human entity, manifesting through the physical body, and transforming utterly. No hierarchical authority can exist or function against the blowing of the spirit.

One final suggestion, which seems inevitable, is that the subsequent destruction of the kingdom, in which Arthur and his knights are defeated after the quest, is the result of their seeking the Grail. That this destruction should arise through Arthur's own seed in the form of his magically inspired offspring of incest is hardly surprising, if we follow the con-cepts of genetic magic through carefully.

The willed pursuit of the power of the spirit brings break-down and change (Matthew X:34), and in the earliest version of the Grail quest, the vessel was stolen from the Underworld, the realm of seething, ever-changing energy. Unless this energy is contained by perfect balance and purity within the outer world, it will rotate according to cycles of creation and destruction, the only way in which its essential nature may be expressed in manifestation. This cyclical pattern of ancient lore repeats itself in the Grail legends, despite the higher order of Salvation offered by the Saviour.

We are promised, however, that Arthur is not dead, but merely sleeping or waiting within the otherworld for the correct time to return. Not wise, indeed, to seek the grave of any of our true kings, virgins or heroes, for they live on within each and every one of us, waiting to be aroused by the power of the spirit, the regeneration offered through the Holy Grail.

Notes

1. For those who seek academic cross references, such delights occur in abundance in the footnotes of any good research work upon medieval or traditional tales. For the present a short list of works is here appended. All have been used extensively in the preparation of this essay. P. Matarasso, *The Quest of The Holy Grail*, Harmondsworth, Penguin, 1969 (translation). J. Cable, *The Death of King Arthur*, Harmondsworth, Penguin, 1971 (translation). J. Gantz, *The Mabinogion*, Harmondsworth, Penguin, 1976 (translation). Rev. C. C. Dobson, *Did Our Lord Visit Britain?*, London, Covenant, 1974. H. Jennings, *The Rosicrucians*, London, George Routledge, 1907. Rev. R. Kirk, *The Secret Commonwealth*, ed. Sanderson, Cambridge, N.J., Brewer/Rowman & Littlefield, 1976. A. and B. Rees, *Celtic Heritage*, Thames & Hudson, London, 1978. A. Ross, *Pagan Celtic Britain*, Cardinal, London, 1974. A. Ross, *Folklore of the Scottish Highlands*, Batsford, London, 1976. H. M. Porter, *The Celtic Church in Somerset*, Morgan, Bath, 1971. E. Pagels, *The Gnostic Gospels*, Weidenfeld & Nicolson, London, 1980. R. Steiner, *The Occult Significance of Blood*, Steiner Publishing Co., London. G. R. S. Mead, *The Hymn of Jesus*, Watkins, London, 1963. L. C. Wimberley, *Folklore in the English and Scottish Ballads*, Ungar, New York, 1959.

2. Matarasso, *op. cit.*, pp. 222–35. The position of this legend relative to the other material of *The Quest* is interesting, for it comes almost as a retrospective key to many of the events and relationships in the preceding adventures. In this key explanatory role, it prepares the reader for the revelations that are to follow.

References

1. Barfield, Owen. *Saving the Appearances*, Wesleyan University Press, Connecticut, 1988.

2. Stewart, R. J. *Earth Light*, Element Books, Shaftesbury, 1992. Also *The Underworld Initiation*, Aquarian Press, Wellingborough, 1985 (available from Sulis Music, BCM 3721, London, WC1N 3XX).

3. Stewart, R. J. *The Waters of the Gap*, Ashgrove Press, Bath, 1990.

4. Masson, Jeffrey. *Against Therapy*, Fontana, London, 1990.

5. Kirk, Robert. *The Secret Commonwealth of Elves, Fauns, and Faeries*. New edition in modern English with commentary by R. J. Stewart, published as *Robert Kirk, Walker Between Worlds*, Element Books, Shaftesbury, 1990.

6. Stewart, R. J. *Living Magical Arts*, Blandford Press, London, 1987 and 1991. Also *Advanced Magical Arts*, Element Books, Shaftesbury, 1988.

7. Stewart, R. J. *The Way of Merlin*, Aquarian Press, London, 1991. Also *The Mystic Life of Merlin* and *The Prophetic Vision of Merlin*, Penguin Arkana, London, 1986; both volumes in single combined edition, 1993.

8. Stewart, R. J. *Psychology and the Spiritual Traditions* (ed.), Element Books, Shaftesbury, 1990.

9. Stewart, R. J. *The Complete Merlin Tarot*, Aquarian Press, London, 1992 (an expanded edition of *The Merlin Tarot*, 1988).

10. Matthews, J. *The Household of the Grail*, Aquarian Press, London, 1990. Also *The Celtic Shaman*, Element Books, 1991.

11. Spangler, D. and Thompson, I. T. *Reimagination of the World*, Bear & Co, Santa Fe, New Mexico, 1991.

12. Stewart, R. J. *Celtic Gods, Celtic Goddesses*, Blandford Press, London, 1989.

Glossary

Adept: one who is skilled in the arts of exchanging consciousness and energy between differing worlds (not a formal grade or qualification).

Allies: beings that work with or assist humans to exchange energies and move between differing worlds.

Ancestor: usually any human from your genetic predecessors, but may also include faery and spiritual beings connected to specific families.

Angels: spiritual messengers, not present in the Underworld but see Figures 11 and 5.

Apollo: originally the Divine Child of the Underworld, embodying therapy, prophecy, music. Later developed as formal deity known from classical Greece. Bridges between Celtic and Classical mythology.

Archangels: spiritual enablers or matrices for energy, not present in the Underworld but see Figures 11 and 5.

Challenging: traditional exchange of greetings, tests and forms of communication.

Cities, the Four: Falias, Murias, Finias, Gorias. Four realms of faery power in the Four Directions (see *Earth Light*).

Companions: may be companion creatures, such as animals, birds or fishes. More powerful companions are beings of the faery and elemental realms; traditionally these beings attend the Sleepers.

Conditions, The Three: three relative states of consciousness within the Underworld (see Figure 5).

Convocations: gatherings of beings with shared modes of awareness, usually encountered as mythic assemblies or ongoing meetings. Typical examples are the mixture of beings in a faery court, or the Company of the Grail. Not identical to Orders, which have special functions.

Co-walkers: faery allies that associate closely with humans. Other allies are not always co-walkers.

Creatures, companion: animals, birds, fishes that work with humans. These are called spiritual animals, though the first level of contact is with creatures of your own land. Another level finds creatures of other lands, and (less common) creatures with no current physical expression.

Dimension: loosely used to mean a metaphysical world found through a change of the direction of attention. Not used in a theoretical sense.

Directions, the Seven: Above, Below, Within, Before, Behind, Right and Left. Aligned with planetary directions of Above, Below, Within, East, West, South, and North. See Figure 11.

Earth Light: the light of universal being active within the Underworld.

Elementals: beings comprised of harmonics of one Element: Air, Fire, Water or Earth.

Ex-humans: beings within the Underworld who once lived as humans on the surface world. Traditionally these are (a) *physically* transported into an Underworld or faery realm, or (b) pass into such realms after physical death keeping full memory, usually due to skill in Underworld disciplines. Should not be confused with the more widespread idea of the spirits of the dead in religion or folklore.

Faeries: the first race of Underworld beings, closest to humans but of prehuman origins.

Falias: (see *Cities*).

Guardian: may be any entity which guards the threshold between the worlds. The Guardian is the Horned God of the ancients, Pan or Cernunnos, associated with powers of life and death, and the protection and purification of living creatures.

Guide: any creature or being that works to guide travellers through the Underworld. May have no other function, or may be a co-walker, companion, ally and so forth. Initial guides are usually spiritual animals or other creatures.

Harmonic (as in musical harmonics or overtones):   a pattern which relates to another pattern in an organic or proportional manner.

Hearing (also **Listening**):   used to mean attuning meditative awareness to streams or emissions of consciousness that take form as words.

Initiation: beginning. The Underworld Initiation is the first step in Underworld work. (Does not involve formal joining of a group or society.)

Kirk, Robert: seventeenth century explorer and chronicler of Gaelic faery traditions. Said to be one of the teachers of faery lore who still contacts seers and listeners today.

Lucifer: the universal Light inherent within the body of the Earth. Traditionally this also refers to an archangelic or stellar being with an individual consciousness. This being is of a prehuman cycle of existence, and related in mystical tradition and folklore to the creation of other prehuman races such as faery beings. Later identification of Lucifer with Satan or evil are not found in the Underworld tradition, which is essentially preChristian and primal Christian, without subsequent orthodox propaganda. We might presume that the name *Lucifer* and its equation with evil was used collectively to denigrate the pagan gods of light in the diverse mythology of the early Christian period.

Mabon: the Celtic name for the Child of Light, related to or identical with the young Apollo. Mabon/Apollo is the god that shines through the youthful prophetic Merlin in Celtic tradition.

Masking: a process in which one form overlays another, with a being appearing at first as something else. The human personality (*persona*) or mask is an obvious example.

Mediating: relaying a spiritual power actively with full awareness through one's self. Not to be confused with mediumship or channelling which are passive.

Merlin: the prophet and awakened Sleeper of the Northern hemisphere.

Mirroring: the reflection and polarization of forms and energies between the surface and Underworld.

Mystery: a pattern or convocation which transforms the initiate. Not always associated with formal or ancient Mystery cults.

Narrative: a defined story and set of images designed to transform the participants. (See also *Visualization*.)

Octave/s: the law of octaves reveals that energies and/or events are reiterated in the proportion 2:1. Musical examples are notes with the same name (i.e. a,b,c) but one or more octaves apart (high and low a,b,c, etc.).

Orders: usually used to mean specific groups of beings in the Underworld with specific functions or self-declared aims.

People:

Places: the three parts of any Mystery.

Powers:

Realm: usually a sub-part of a world: thus the faery realm is a part of the Underworld, but not all of it.

Redeemer: Christ, and other sacrificial redemptive figures in spiritual lore.

Regeneration: the process and result of Underworld transformation: the breakdown of the conditioned delusions of selfhood to be reharmonized in a new pattern.

Reversion: a temporary return to an earlier psychic state or condition, as experienced during the regeneration process of the Underworld Initiation.

Revision: memory and re-experience of deep patterns within the present life cycle which are carried over from apparently past lives. Past lives are remembered and revised as a result of entering the Underworld.

Rhymer, Thomas: a thirteenth century Scottish poet and prophet. Traditionally still in the faery realm, and said to contact seers, poets and initiates. Like Robert Kirk (see above), is said to be one of an order of ex-humans within the Underworld.

Sacred Space: the acknowledging and opening of the Seven Directions into other worlds.

Seeing: as in seership, involves the Second Sight and powerful Underworld visions. Not to be confused with popular clairvoyance.

Seer: one who can consciously see at will into the Underworld, or who sees Underworld and faery beings when they cross into the human world. A seer may also be able to see into other dimensions that are not of the human or Underworld.

Silence, the: a state of inner stillness and poise, approached through regular meditation.

Sleeper: a potent but dormant spiritual being embodied within (a) a locality such as a sacred site, (b) the land, (c) a planetary zone, and (d) the planet as a whole.

Temples: locations and energy patterns which act as exchanges between the worlds. Many temples exist in the Underworld or other worlds in addition to those in the human world.

Testing: a process of challenge, riddling or trickery, often found during early encounters with faery and Underworld contacts.

Three Worlds, the: Moon, Sun and Star. Represented by the three Tarot trumps of the same name and defined by the *Axis Mundi* or pivot of the worlds. Three relative spatial, energetic and conscious states, with expressions as the Earth and Moon, Solar System, and Galaxy.

Underworld journey: any conscious entry into and return from the Underworld.

Utterances: manifestations of universal power as limited forms.

Vision: the inner or fundamental element of an empowered visualization or visionary text.

Visualization, empowered: a visual sequence (with or without words) used to attune consciousness/energy to specific spiritual places, people and powers.

Watchers: beings who watch from locations or thresholds, and relay what they see. Traditionally a feature of faery and Underworld lore.

Index

EARTH LIGHT

The Ancient Path to Transformation

*Rediscovering the Wisdom of
Celtic and Faery Lore*

R J Stewart

The Underworld Tradition, clearly defined in ancient Celtic sources, is a transformatory initiatory system involving a mysterious realm hidden deep within our human consciousness.

EARTH LIGHT explains that through working with the powerful techniques of visualization and imagination, a vital key to gaining a true understanding of ourselves can be found.

Price: £9.99 $15.95 ISBN: 1 85230 243 7

THE ELEMENTS OF
PROPHECY

R J Stewart

Prophecy is an inherent potential of the human psyche and culture. This book brings the subject out of the realms of superstition and into the grasp of the reader.

Price: £4.99 $8.95 ISBN: 1 85230 134 1

THE ELEMENTS OF
CREATION MYTH

R J Stewart

An introduction to the many similarities in different cultures' creation myths and their symbolism.

Price: £4.99 $8.95 ISBN: 1 85230 106 6